The Gift of

Encouraging Words

The Gift of Encouraging Words

reflections from the
writings of

Florence Littauer

WORD PUBLISHING
Dallas•London•Vancouver•Melbourne

THE GIFT OF ENCOURAGING WORDS

Unless otherwise indicated, all Scripture quotations in this volume are from the King James Version of the Bible.

Scripture references indicated NKJV are from the New King James Version, copyright © 1979, 1980, 1982, 1990, Thomas Nelson, Inc., Publisher. Reprinted by permission.

Scripture references indicated NIV are from the New International Version, copyright © 1983 by the International Bible Society. Used by permission of Zondervan Bible Publishers.

Scripture references indicated TEV are from Today's English Version (the *Good News Bible*) Old Testament © 1976 by the American Bible Society; New Testament © 1966, 1971, 1976 by the American Bible Society. Used by permission.

Scripture references indicated TLB are from *The Living Bible* (Wheaton, Illinois: Tyndale House Publishers, 1971). Used by permission.

Library of Congress Cataloging-in-Publication Data
Littauer, Florence, 1928-
  The gift of encouraging words / Florence Littauer.
    p. cm.
  ISBN 0-8499-1206-7
  1. Encouragement—Religious aspects—Christianity—Meditations.
  2. Devotional calendars. I. Title.
  BV4647.E53L56 1995
  242—dc20
                                                        95-19894
                                                        CIP

Printed in the United States of America
5 6 7 8 9 BVG 9 8 7 6 5 4 3 2 1

Contents

Therefore encourage each other with these words.

1 Thessalonians 4:18 NIV

❧

There are some who stand surefooted on the shore, ready to throw a large smooth stone into the pond of life, knowing the waves of it will wash a crest of joy over all of us who wade in the shallows, waiting for a word of encouragement.

There are some who hold their stones to be so precious, they could not drop even a tiny gem into the water for fear it would sink unnoticed and disappear before the owner received even a glance of approval for his generosity. They leave us empty-handed.

Then there are those who for some reason unknown to them or to those of us observing, have neither a smooth stone nor a faceted gem but hold a palmful of pitiful pebbles with little promise and yet throw out one a day in hopes that a small ripple of pleasure will reach a stranded soul in need of a smile. Through His love and power, they give us all they have, and it is enough—for they have given us the gift of encouraging words.

A Hidden Letter

A young lady came to me with a tale of hostility toward her husband. As she poured out all his misdeeds, they seemed so trivial that I asked her when her feelings of hatred had started. She replied quickly, "I was mad at him before we even got married."

Her fiancé had written a letter instructing her to find a car for their honeymoon trip. She had answered that it was his responsibility to provide transportation, and besides, his family had three cars while hers had only one. He made it clear: "If you want to marry me, you had better find a car!" She found a car, but she vowed she would never forget his injustice.

She looked up at me with bitterness lining her face and said, "In case you don't believe me, I'll show you the letter he wrote." She reached into her handbag and pulled out a worn and tattered envelope that had moved from bag to bag for ten years. As she handed it to me, she said, "I always carry it with me so I won't forget."

Probably none of us has a letter like this in our handbags, but we may have one in our heads. How can God work in a heart hardened with hatred? How can we ever know joy when we are busy recording indelibly our partner's mistakes?

God warns us that bitterness can defile or destroy a person's life. Hebrews 12:14–15 says, "Pursue peace with all people, and holiness, without which no one will see the Lord: looking carefully lest anyone fall short of the grace of God; lest any root of bitterness springing up cause trouble, and by this many become defiled" (NKJV).

It is easy to see that this woman's bitterness had given full birth to hatred. We must not allow bitterness to take root. We must learn to be transparent when we've truly been hurt. We need to be willing to forgive our mates (and others) in order to keep our hearts cleansed from bitterness.

Bitterness is a poison (Acts 8:23) and one of Satan's most subtly deceptive means of destroying marriages. Next time you feel that twinge of resentment, stop and decide not to "put that letter in your purse."

꧁

Do you have a "letter" in your head? Ask the Father to forgive your unforgiveness and bitterness. Ask the Holy Spirit to help you forgive your offender and to help you stand against being offended in the future. Tear up the letter and begin to allow the Lord to cause your hardened heart to soften and His joy to return.

We Are His Expression

First Timothy 5:10 states, "Relieve the afflicted." To make sure I understood the meaning clearly I looked in the dictionary. *Relieve* means "to free from pain or embarrassment." The *afflicted* are "those depressed with continued suffering, misfortune, or calamity."

The easiest reaction to trauma in others is to ignore it. That way you don't have to get yourself involved in something difficult to handle. In crisis times more people choose the ignore-the-problem method than any other. If you look the other way, it may go away. It may, but not because of you. I have talked to so many women who in times of trauma were virtually abandoned by their friends and church. No one wants to see the retarded child; no one wants to get involved in the divorce; no one knows what to do with a rape victim; no one enjoys weepy widows or dying cancer patients. It's so much easier to look the other way. Yet how do you feel when you are the victim? Do you feel like you have leprosy and have been abandoned?

The traumas of life aren't popular, and it is much easier to handle new babies and broken legs. Yet if you and I are to *relieve* the afflicted we must try to ease their pain and not embarrass them. You and I must love the unlovable and help anyone we know who is distressed or depressed. We are the hands God uses to hold the hurting. We are the feet that help carry the loads that are too heavy. We are the tangible manifestation of the compassionate heart of our Father. You and I are the expression of God's love on this earth.

❧

Choose today to meditate on 1 Timothy 5:10 and take it to heart. The world will truly notice a difference when you are compassionate to the afflicted. The world has become very cold to the hurts of people. Therefore, it is imperative that we as Christians be different and genuinely care for others.

Affirmation Habitation

Wives, do you make your husband feel that he is the most important person in life to you? So many men are in a period labeled "midlife crisis." They feel useless and worthless. They look around at a busy wife and children who ignore them, they sense their job is going nowhere, and they say, "Is this all there is to life?" Wives can help prevent this devastation by renewing their goal of putting their husbands first.

A husband so often takes his wife for granted. He doesn't realize how dull her life seems compared to the magazines touting the superwoman success. She gets no pay for laundry and dishes; she has no hope for advancement. As her husband, can you let her know you appreciate her efforts? Can you take the burden of the children at least once a week? Can you uplift her, encourage her, and help her? Can you make her feel special?

It is also very important that we affirm our children. We must develop that inner attitude of loving affirmation within our homes. If our mates and children don't receive affirmation at home, more than likely they will look for it elsewhere. Let's make our homes that secure refuge of affirmation.

No matter who we are, we need to be affirmed—we need to feel special! We must first allow the Father God to affirm us. In order to receive affirmation from

God we must first truly know that He loves us unconditionally and has our best interest at heart. We must know that the Father believes us and has uniquely designed and uniquely destined you for a particular plan and purpose on this earth! He made you to be you! Now that's affirming! As you receive affirmation from God, you will be able to pour out unconditional love and affirmation to your spouse. Know that you are accepted by God and allow the Lord to pour His love through you to your mate.

"To the praise of the glory of His grace, by which he made us accepted in the Beloved" (Ephesians 1:6 NKJV).

❦

Do you tend to be critical of your mate? What about your children? Do you make them feel rejected? Begin by going to the Father God so that He can affirm you. Then ask the Holy Spirit to help you be a vessel of affirmation to your family and friends.

My Desires Will Be His Desires

Shortly after Fred and I became believing Christians and before we had any idea God was much more than a reason to go to church on Sunday, we went to the country club one Saturday evening. The club was the center of our social life, and we always attended the weekend parties and formal dances. This one evening we were sitting at our usual table with our usual friends when suddenly I saw the setting as if for the first time. The conversation seemed pointless and the people pathetic. I realized they had all been drinking too much and weren't even making sense. Since we had always been considered squares because we didn't drink, we had tried to be the life of the party and go along with their behavior no matter what it was. This charade had never bothered me because I wanted so much to be an accepted part of the club elite.

I can picture that evening with Fred looking movie-star handsome in his tuxedo and me in one of my many gowns. The man next to me, whom I knew well, had his arm around me and was noisily kissing my shoulder. Suddenly he looked pitiful, and I had an urge to push him off his chair. I glanced across at Fred, and a voluptuous, tipsy woman was hanging on him and batting her false eyelashes up and down in his face. These flirting actions were probably the same that night as they'd been many times before, but I saw them with new eyes. I had no idea why things looked different to me at that time, but as I listened to the same music and stared at the same walls, I wanted to run. I asked myself, "What in the world are we doing here?"

In the car going home I sighed to Fred, "Do you know what thought went through my head tonight?" Before I got any further he added, "Let me guess because it might be the same as mine. I looked around at the people and the place and asked myself, 'What in the world are we doing here?'" I screamed in excitement over our identical thoughts, and if the angel Gabriel had suddenly appeared on the hood of our car, we could not have been more spiritually moved. God had spoken to us both at the same time with the same message. On the way home we agreed not to return to the club, and we never went back again. God didn't forbid us from going there or burn the club down; He just changed our desires.

God is so faithful to meet us where we are in our lives. Once we receive Christ into our hearts as Savior, the Holy Spirit begins to teach us how to make Him Lord of every area of our lives. As we become intimate with Him, His desires will become our desires.

Communication Closeness

When we are dating we feel free to converse because we know the other person will receive our words with an open mind. We want to get to know each other and listen with attention. But as we begin to function in the closeness of marriage, we begin to find negative reactions to some of our favorite subjects. The more fearful we become of pushing our partner in an adverse direction, the less we communicate. Because we are afraid of a bad reaction, we tend to share our true feelings with outsiders who will listen. This can cause problems within a relationship.

The majority of the couples I counsel don't hate each other but are just emotionally divorced. They stopped *communicating* somewhere along the line, and neither side did anything about it. Don't let this happen to you. Don't wait for your wife to become hysterical; plan relaxing times when you can get away together and communicate. Don't take friends or relatives along or go on a tour with twenty-four-hour activities. Go to a quiet motel and renew acquaintances.

One night Fred said, "We haven't had enough time to converse with each other. Let's set aside the hour after dinner and go to our room alone."

"You mean before you do your telephone counseling?" I asked. The first night I talked nonstop for over an hour, the second night an hour, the third night thirty minutes, and by the fourth night I didn't have much to say. It was amazing how my feelings changed. Once I knew Fred would listen, I no longer had a compulsion to converse. That step on Fred's part tore down resentment I had built up and removed the barrier in our communication.

Some of you may have spent so many years building your walls of defensiveness to cordon off your own area of private property that it would take King Arthur and his entire court to knock down your fortress. You have learned how to fend off invaders with your weapons, and you've successfully kept your mate at a distance. You communicate on your terms on your topics at your time. And this will not work!

You must be willing to take the necessary step, not waiting for your mate to make the move. It is vital to keep the communication line open. Take the time and make the effort. It will be worth it.

❧

Even if your communication is good in your relationship, sit down and discuss the topic with your mate—and listen to his perception of your relationship's communication. Some couples who do not force themselves to sit down and discuss their communication never know there's a problem until it is too late.

Who's in Charge?

Because Fred and I both have the powerful Choleric temperament and like to be in charge, our marriage had many problems in the area of control. When this happens in a relationship, there are different ways of dealing with the situation.

One, the stronger of the two takes over and dictates how the other will behave, leading to a boss/slave relationship that will ultimately blow up. Two, the partners live separate lives with different careers and see as little as possible of each other. This method maintains decorum but leads to emotional divorce. Three, they both force themselves to give in to the other in an effort to be loving, selfless Christians. However, neither one will make a decision, and the stalemate makes them both so impatient and angry that they can't stand to be together. Four, they set some common goals, list the necessary steps to get there, and then divide the responsibilities.

Fred and I have tried all of the possibilities, and only number four works. Before Fred gave up his business to travel and speak with me, we were alternating between number two and number three! Using number four we sat down and made a list of all the different aspects of a traveling ministry and took turns choosing which duties we would assume. The next step was more difficult, remembering to be responsible for our own list and not checking up on each other. We had agreed that Fred was in charge of schedules, fees, book sales, and the office staff. One day I came in and reprimanded a worker for not putting things away in the right places. Fred called me into his room and asked me if I would like to run the office. "Oh no!" I replied. "Then don't tell the staff what to do," he said. "If there's something wrong, tell me and I will take care of it. The office is on my list. Remember?" I've remembered.

Because we have taken the time to delineate the responsibilities and follow through on our own choices, we have eliminated strife and can travel together twenty-five days a month and enjoy the company.

We know who is in charge. We *both* are in charge, but of *different* things.

❧

Do you find yourself wanting to be in control of everything, including your mate, your job, etc.? Take a practical approach today and sit down and make a list like Fred and I did. Pray and acknowledge God's sovereign control in your life and then ask the Holy Spirit to help you relinquish those things of which you are not in charge.

Different by Design!

Fred and I spent the first fifteen years of our marriage trying to change each other. I thought if only he would loosen up, laugh occasionally, and have fun, I could be happy. He was thinking if only she'd get serious, be on time, and check off the charts I've so carefully made for her, there might be some hope. We didn't understand each other, and even though we never yelled at one another, we were miserable inside. We knew how to do the right things, belong to the right clubs, live on the right side of town, and raise the right kind of children. But our right plans turned wrong when we produced two sons, one after another, who were born with a fatal brain defect.

Suddenly we faced a reality we had never antici-pated. Keeping quiet about our differences and pre-tending to be happy didn't work anymore. At that point, fifteen years into a businesslike marriage, two things happened. One, we both committed our lives to the Lord Jesus in a personal and meaningful way, and two, we started a study of the four basic tempera-ments. I found out that I was the popular Sanguine who wanted to have fun, and Fred was the perfect Melancholy who was depressed if all of life didn't add up in perfect columns. We both were also part of the powerful Choleric who wants to be in charge. I wanted to be in control and enjoy life. Fred wanted to be in charge and make everything and everyone perfect. What a blessing it was to find that we were born with different personalities and that different wasn't wrong. As soon as we accepted each other as we were, we invited couples into our home and began to teach them what we'd learned. We saw marriages changed right there in our living room. Soon we were asked to share in our church, and that was the beginning of a ministry that has spread around the world and spawned over twenty books on getting along with people who are nothing like us!

⚜

Have you seen your mate's differences as something negative? Have you ever stopped to realize that God put the two of you together to "complete" each other?

Thank the Father today for making your mate (or children or coworkers) different than He made you. Make a commitment to gain understanding about the different temperaments and how they affect your relationships. Ask the Father to illuminate the strengths of others whose personalities are different from yours.

Affirmed by the Father God

From the time I was a child I remember seeking my mother's approval. I always did well in everything I tackled, and I knew enough not to attempt sports, art, or music because I had no talent in these areas. My mind could learn the rules, principles, or keyboard, but my body wouldn't cooperate. My mother, a violin and cello teacher, was disappointed that I couldn't even hold the bow correctly, so I set out to excel where I could. I got good grades and hoped that Mother would praise me. Once when I asked her why she did not tell other people how well I was doing in school after my friend Peggy's mother had bragged about her, she replied, "You never know when you'll have to eat your words."

Throughout life I've tried to pull a compliment out of Mother, but while she was never negative, she hung in at neutral. One day within the past few years, I came home after a frustrating visit. I'd shown Mother my exciting schedule of speaking, including a European trip, a Cancun retreat, and an Alaskan cruise. Her response was, "It's amazing you're so busy considering what you do is something nobody needs."

I was discouraged and told Fred of the comment. He looked up and said, "When are you going to grow up and be able to function without your mother's approval?" I was shocked at this question. I *was* grown up, and my success *didn't* depend on my mother's approval—or did it?

Fred continued, "How old is your mother?" "Eighty-five," I responded. "Has she praised you much before?" Fred questioned. "No," I sighed.

With a gentle firmness Fred said, "Then what makes you think she'll start today? If she hasn't been excited about your life before, what makes you expect she'll change now? Why don't you stop trying to impress her, and just love her as she is? Isn't that what you teach others?"

I wish I could say I enjoyed Fred's analysis and that I was so spiritual I leaped at his solution. Instead, I just kept quiet and thought about it. But the more I thought about it, the more I realized he was right. My mother is a Phlegmatic personality not given to enthusiasm and applause for what I do. How childish of me, understanding the different temperaments well, to be seeking something from my mother that is against her nature.

As the truth sank into me, I realized a principle in getting along with people: We should give them what they desire and not be looking for them to fill our needs.

❧

Maybe you have been looking for someone to fill the need of affirmation in your life. Let the Father God affirm you so you won't be seeking the approval of people. When we are affirmed in who we are in Jesus Christ, we can freely and unconditionally love others.

Patchwork "Guilts"

Is there a spiritual way to handle guilt? Yes, there is—
I've used it.

First we must divide our guilt into two categories.
Ask God to bring to your mind the things you feel
guilty about and write them down. Keep writing until
you can't think of anything more. Now go back over
the list. After each item ask yourself, "Do I feel guilty
about this because I really am guilty? Are my emotions
justified? Have I really done something wrong?" Where
the answer is yes, put a checkmark.

Perhaps you are depressed by some guilt you know
you could do something about. Look over your list and
get moving.

How much of your guilt is unnecessary? Are people
expecting more of you than you can handle? Are people pressuring you into positions you have no time for?
Are people judging you according to their own narrow
standards?

You can't please everyone. You can only do the best
you know how to under the circumstances and not
worry about what people think. Ask the Lord right
now to remove all the guilt that has been put upon you
by other people.

There is nothing we can do about changing others'
behavior, but we can deal with unnecessary guilt in a
spiritual way. When someone tries to make you feel

guilty, thank him for the suggestion and tell him you will certainly give it serious consideration. If it has merit, think about it; if it does not, ask the Lord to quickly remove even the memory of the statement from you.

Before you go any further, make sure you have looked over those patchwork "guilts" that are covering up your joy. Then ask the Lord to fold them up and put them away in a distant closet. Believe Him when He says they are gone. Don't go hunting for them again. They're the Lord's property. And we have the promise in Hebrews 9:14 that He will make our consciences clean.

Claim this scripture for yourself today:

❧

How much more shall the blood of Christ, who through the eternal Spirit offered Himself without spot to God, purge your conscience from dead works to serve the living God?" (Hebrews 9:14 NKJV).

Thank You, Father, for freedom from guilt through Jesus. Amen.

Content in California

According to the dictionary, maturity is "a growing up, a completeness, a ripening, a full development." Most of us feel that we've grown up and have completed something. A better way to check our maturity is to ask, "Have we learned to accept responsibility and adjust to our situations?"

When God directed our family to leave Connecticut, where we had lived for thirteen years, to move into the desert of California, I was brokenhearted. I was very new in my Christian faith, and I had not experienced God's firm direction and constant care for me. All I could see was the leaving of a secure situation for an uncertain future. I didn't know enough about the Bible to realize that when God wanted to teach people lessons, He often sent them to deserts. As I sat sadly in San Bernardino studying God's Word, I found Paul's verse on maturity in Philippians 4:11: "I have learned, in whatsoever state I am, therewith to be content."

Did this mean that I should be content in the state of California? Yes. Could I leave lush, green Connecticut with its assets and be happy in the desert of California with its uncertainties? Paul said that he had to *learn* to be content. It didn't come easily. I determined to learn to be content in California. That agreement with God was my first step in growing up. I must learn in whatever circumstances I am to be content.

Maturity comes when we are able to accept our present position in life and adjust to our situation with gratitude. We need to praise the Lord anyhow!

❧

God will be faithful to us. We must make the choice to learn to be content—regardless of the circumstances or situations. When we learn the secret of contentment (whatever the "state"!), we will be walking in a maturity ripe with the fruit of peace and joy.

Memorize and meditate on Philippians 4:11–13 NKJV: "Not that I speak in regard to need, for I have learned in whatever state I am, to be content: I know how to be abased, and I know how to abound. Everywhere and in all things I have learned both to be full and to be hungry, both to abound and to suffer need. I can do ALL THINGS through Christ who strengthens me." (emphasis mine)

The Problem Promise

As we reflect on our lives, we see that we have each had a beginning, each fallen into some kind of trouble, each tried to find a way out. Just as the Hebrews in Egyptian slavery were trying to escape, so are we seeking solutions for our problems. As they were looking for a savior, so we are looking for a God who will set us free.

There are many avenues that we can pursue to gain greater understanding of the problems we face that keep us from being free. The outside help we find is a tool in God's hands to encourage us or give us deeper insight. However, the ultimate answer always rests in His Word and in the transforming love of God. ". . . God is faithful, who will not allow you to be tempted beyond what you are able, but with the temptation will also make the way of escape, that you may be able to bear it" (1 Corinthians 10:13 NKJV).

If I had written the Bible I would have put things differently: I would have given each committed believer an easy life. But God did not see it my way; He planned life on earth to be a testing ground for our future. As a parent corrects a child he loves, God chastens us for our own good. He allows us to go through trials to perfect our character.

Therefore, we don't need to try to squirm out of our difficulties, but face them—knowing that God is faithful and that He will not allow us to be tested too far. He does not promise us a rose garden, but He does say that with the trial He will provide us a way of escape. When I first read that word "escape" I was encouraged. God was going to help me run away from my problems, skirt around them, or tunnel under them; but then I looked at the last clause: "that you may be able to bear it." To bear anything you have to stay with it. These thoughts seemed contradictory, so I hunted up the word "escape" in its original use and found that it means to be lifted above the problem enough to get a more detached perspective. This escape is what God has for us. He will pick us up from the depth of our depression and give us an objective view of our situation so that we will be able to bear it, not run away from it.

As we overcome each trial through God's power and grace, we will see that we can be "free" regardless of the circumstances around us. God will set our feet on high places so we can bear any situation we must face.

❧

Are your problems causing you to want to duck your head and run? Do you need God to pick you up and give you a different perspective so that you can face any situation? Ask the Lord to set your feet on high places today. Read Psalm 18:16–33 for a good dose of encouragement for any problem you may be facing.

A Fruity Character

When we find God, others will notice a change. Not only will we look more radiant as we reflect the Lord's glory, but also the Holy Spirit, the power and energy of the Trinity, will transform us into the likeness of Christ. Bit by bit there will be changes as we commit our lives to Jesus and obey His will for us.

We will begin to manifest the fruit of the Spirit. As we stand in the presence of God we will have more *love* for others than we ever thought was possible. We will be able to exhibit the *joy* of the Lord even in adverse circumstances. The *peace* that passes all understanding will keep our hearts and minds safe in Christ Jesus. *Patience* that we never had will come over us in a wave of compassion and understanding for those we could barely tolerate before. An attitude of relaxed *kindness* to others will replace our self-seeking natures, and a real *goodness,* a true desire to help without thought of human credit, will become apparent to those we meet. For some of us who have wavered in our dedication to God in the past, the gift of *faithfulness* will be added, and people will see that we've been with Jesus. There will be a new *gentleness,* a softness in our faces and in our actions that will attract people to us, and we will gain a *self-control* over some of our habits and tempers that have hindered others from seeking the Lord.

After we have accepted Jesus as our Savior and

Lord, the fruit of the Spirit (love, joy, peace, patience, kindness, goodness, faithfulness, gentleness, and self-control) is already in us! We just have to spend time in the presence of the Lord and His Word so that we can allow it to come up out of our spirit! Therefore, it is not as difficult as one would think. As we learn to walk in the power of the Holy Spirit, the fruit of the Spirit will be manifest in our character. The more time we spend with the Lord, the more of His character we will radiate!

Meditate and memorize Galatians 5:22–23 and ask the Holy Spirit to help you develop the fruit of the Spirit in your life.

"But the fruit of the Spirit is love, joy, peace, longsuffering, kindness, goodness, faithfulness, gentleness, self-control. Against such there is no law" (NKJV).

Irresistible Beauty

There is little hope for us to have happy husbands when we are belligerent and domineering. When we preach liberation and are trying to find ourselves, it is difficult for our men to want to be the sweet Christians that we want them to be. Yet when we aim to please, our husbands see a spirit in us that is hard to resist. We can win them over by our conduct. We won't have to say a word. Yet how can we walk in that kind of love?

It is impossible to love our husbands fully until we love the Lord. When we can communicate on a personal level with the Lord, we can hope to be in tune with our husbands. *Redbook* magazine, in one of its many surveys, proclaimed on the cover, "Religious Women Make Better Lovers." While the writers couldn't put their finger on the reason, they had to conclude that those women surveyed who had a "strong faith" were more happily married.

When we start each day talking quietly with the Lord, we're less apt to scream at our husbands. When we keep our eyes looking up instead of around, we're not going to keep a record of wrongs. When we're able to see our husbands' inner self, we're not so concerned with physique. When we do all things heartily as unto the Lord (Colossians 3:23), we consider housework an investment in marriage.

So why are religious women better lovers? Because

they love the Lord, have submissive attitudes toward their husbands, and are aiming for quiet, gentle spirits that are of great value in the sight of God and man. A quiet and gentle spirit does not mean that you are a doormat or never talk. It is an issue of the heart that makes a woman beautiful. There is power, strength, and beauty in a woman who chooses to love the Lord with all her heart and allows the Holy Spirit to help her walk in a quiet and gentle spirit.

❦

Do not let your adornment be merely outward— arranging the hair, wearing gold, or putting on fine apparel—rather let it be the hidden person of the heart, with the incorruptible beauty of a gentle and quiet spirit, which is very precious in the sight of God (1 Peter 3:3–4 NKJV).

Ask the Lord to make you beautiful today— from the inside out! Ask the Holy Spirit to help you yield your heart so that you will have a gentle and quiet spirit.

A Secret about Women

We women want so much to be loved. We want our man to put his arms around us, to comfort us, to speak kindly to us, to care for us. Men, if we know you love us, we can put up with other discomforts, but if we are not sure, we will ask for the moon to test you. Do you see a pattern here?

When you criticize us, we get worse.

When you compliment us, we get better.

When you try to change us, we won't budge.

When you accept us as we are, we try to improve.

*When you don't help us, we're mad because
    you're sitting.*

*When you're willing to assist, we insist that you
    sit down.*

*When you pick on the children, we think you
    hate us.*

*When you are positive and encouraging, we know
    you love us.*

When you are too busy to listen, we nag and ramble.

*When you set aside time to converse, we condense
    our comments.*

We are really so easy to please when you love us. You can turn our whole lives around when you let us know we come first. Let us know that we are precious to you and that we are cherished.

❧

Men, ask God to give you His unconditional love for your wife and children. Ask God to pour His love through you to your family. As you allow yourself to be a vessel through which He loves them, they will bloom like flowers in the garden of your love.

"Husbands, love your wives, just as Christ also loved the church and gave Himself for her, that He might sanctify and cleanse her with the washing of the water by the word, that He might present her to Himself a glorious church, not having spot or wrinkle or any such thing, but that she should be holy and without blemish. So husbands ought to love their own wives as their own bodies he who loves his wife loves himself. For no one ever hated his own flesh, but nourishes and cherishes it, just as the Lord does the church" (Ephesians 5:25–29 NKJV).

Powdered Words

When we are in control of our senses, we can stop damaging words before they get out. Some of us Sanguines (the fun-loving speak-before-you-think temperament!) get our mouth in motion before our brain is in gear, and we live to regret it. We must train ourselves to think before we speak. Once the words are out, we can't stuff them back in—they are intangible, illusive.

On Marita's (our youngest daughter) fourth birthday she received four talcum powder mitts. No child needed that much powder, so I put them away. The following Sunday we had company, and while the adults lingered over dessert the children went to Marita's room to play. After a while a little girl came out ghostly white from head to toe. Only her eyes stood out. The mothers all ran to see what had happened. The children had found the four talcum mitts and they had powdered each other completely. Every particle of powder was out of the mitts and the room was a mist of white. For months when we walked on Marita's carpet little puffs of powder appeared.

Many families have done the same with words. We've covered each other with angry barbs and sarcastic accusations. We've hit each other with demeaning phrases, and we can't get them back. No matter how we try to apologize, those words are out there floating loose. We can't stuff them back in our mitts, and when we tread on certain subjects those words come up as dust between our toes.

Maybe you need to ask your family or others to forgive you for hurting words you have spoken. Even though you cannot take them back, you can ask forgiveness and then ask the Lord to restore the hurts in the relationship.

※

Humble yourself this day and ask the Father to restore fellowship. Oh, dear friends, don't lash out with words you'll have to eat later! Yet if you already have, eat them quickly and restore "the years that the locust hath eaten" (Joel 2:25).

Pray and claim Psalm 141:3 for yourself daily! "Set a guard, O Lord, over my mouth; keep watch over the door of my lips" (NKJV).

Bull's-Eye!

While we can accept that our first human priority is to care for our families, we should open our minds to the fact that *our whole life is a preparation for ministry.* For you young women who are at home with the children, don't let your mind wander out to pasture. Keep alert, keep reading, keep thinking. Know that God has given you a ministry and will expand it when He feels you are ready. Don't wait until you can see the handwriting on the wall; use every available mental moment to *prepare today for God's call tomorrow.*

One summer when I was teaching drama at Camp Trebor, the archery instructor quit. The director asked if anyone could teach the class. No one volunteered even though additional wages sweetened the proposition. I did a quick mental review of my college archery class and raised my hand. Even though I had little athletic ability, I remembered the basic principles of the sport, and I lined the young girls up in the field with their bows and arrows. At first we had no target; the girls had to get the arrow moving and learn the basic skills. When they could simply send the shaft sailing somewhere, we set up a target. Up until then they were playing games, but they didn't have a goal. It's hard to hit the target when you don't have one. As each girl focused in, she narrowed her aim until she found the target. Some hit the straw around the edge, some scored, and a few found the bull's-eye.

Some of us don't want to practice or prepare until the final target is right before us and we can see the bull's-eye, and yet God often does not reveal His ultimate plan until He sees that we are ready. He doesn't reach down for the idle mind, the lazy body, or the empty spirit. He wants someone who's preparing for the future even when she can't see the target.

Today there are so many opportunities for people who are ready. There are so many groups desperate for leaders, so many lonely people craving attention, so many depressed souls waiting for uplifting counsel. Are you ready? Take the time to prepare for leadership—it starts with a desire to learn and the discipline of preparation. Then when the great target appears, you will be able to hit the bull's-eye.

❦

Are you willing to do "what's in your hand"? Are you willing to "pay your dues" to be the leader that God has called you to be? Give God time to build the character in your life that will enable you to be a leader that will bring Him glory.

"Whatever your hand finds to do, do it with your might" (Ecclesiastes 9:10 NKJV).

Graciously Humble

Not one of us wants to be criticized, yet we seem equally uncomfortable with praise. Some of us have been knocked down so long that we don't feel we deserve a compliment, and some of us doubt that any positive person is really telling the truth. Where does this negative attitude place the positive person? How does this kind and uplifting individual feel when he has given a compliment and the recipient's response ranges from uneasy silence to vehement denial?

How would I feel if I saw you in a royal purple gown at the president's reception and said, "What a beautiful gown. You look like a queen in purple!" and you returned, "Look like a queen? Are you crazy? I look more like the maid"? You have now let me know I'm stupid and wouldn't know a queen if I were standing in Buckingham Palace.

How about a hypothetical compliment: "That's a lovely linen suit you're wearing today." Some possible responses:

- "This old thing?"
- "This isn't linen; it's just rayon."
- "I picked it up at Goodwill."
- "It's a reject from my sister."

Any of these comments show I have no taste and

remind me never to say a nice word to you again.

Many wives complain that their husbands never give them compliments. One man summed it up when he said, "I used to tell her how good she looked, and she'd always make me feel like a dummy for saying so. Finally I quit noticing anything, and now she complains."

A dentist complimented his receptionist, "Your hair looks great today."

She retorted, "What was wrong with it yesterday?"

We mean to be humble, but we insult the intelligence of the givers when we refuse their compliments. How much happier we can make others when we express gratitude for their comments. A simple thank you is sufficient, but if you wish to make a positive addition, that is even better.

Accept each compliment as you would a present, words wrapped up in a box with a bow on top. Say thank you and you'll receive more; reject the praise and you'll soon receive none.

❦

Examine your own responses to compliments. Do compliments make you uncomfortable? Are your responses continually negative? Make the choice to respond in gratitude. Begin by allowing the Heavenly Father to fill your heart with gratitude— for out of your heart flow the issues of life.

Think Spots

God has given us the ability to improve our minds and to use the creative thinking that He has given us to impact the world. Yet before we can get down to actually improving our minds, we should set aside some spot where we can think quietly and be uninterrupted. Because we don't take the time and effort to remove ourselves from the confusion of life, we have difficulty doing much creative thinking. The Lord Jesus taught us the value of withdrawing to a quiet place to pray and think. Do you have such a spot? Do you already have a place for your daily quiet time? If not, this might be the start of something new.

Some have a desk, a corner table, an easy chair. One girl I know drives to a camellia garden, one walks by the shore, one sits in her car overlooking the city. My favorite spot is in my bathroom. I have a tub with a carpeted step up to it and I lay my Bible there and sit on the floor. A ledge behind the tub holds pots of African violets, and the window opens into a plant-filled atrium. This spot is beautiful to look at and peaceful to my soul. It is here that I've prayed through some difficult times in my life. It is a special place where I can be still and know that He is Almighty God.

Airplanes are "think spots" for me also. When I finish a seminar and sink into a seat on the plane, I am alone, able to sort out the seminar, able to jot down creative ideas and improvements before I forget them.

Many of you may want to combine your daily devotions with your thinking time. God asks that we put Him first, give Him our first 10 percent. As we pray and read God's Word, we can open our minds to His direction and let His thoughts stimulate ours. "Let this mind be in you, which was also in Christ Jesus" (Philippians 2:5).

As we begin to realize how little time we spend in solitary meditation, is it any wonder our brain is only functioning at one-tenth of its potential? If you wish to speed up your thinking process, start by finding a "think spot" and setting aside time to use it. Once you find how much fun it is to expand your creative ability, you will see "think spots" everywhere: in your car, in line at the supermarket, in the dentist's waiting room, in church. Make use of them, think constantly, and allow the Holy Spirit to ignite the creativity the Lord has placed within you.

※

Maybe it is time you plugged in to the creative juices of the Holy Spirit and put to use the mind that God has blessed you with. Pray for a release of creativity and determine to develop "think spots" in your life this very hour.

Simply Obedient

When my adopted son Fred was eight years old, he got himself in a little trouble at school. He had listened to my teaching on Adam and Eve, so when I questioned him on his trouble, he replied, "If it had not been for Adam and Eve and that apple, I wouldn't be in this mess today!" How true.

How about the rest of us? Are we in a mess today? Are we looking for God to bail us out? Has someone told us that when we ask the Lord into our life it will become a rose garden?

My favorite hymn as a child was "In the Garden" by C. Austin Miles. Because my father's store in which we lived was set right on the sidewalk and our yard was the cracked cement where the one gas pump had settled in, I always longed for green grass and some flowers. I longed to talk with God in a garden like Adam and Eve did when He met with them in the lush Garden of Eden.

God asked simple obedience and honesty in return for fellowship and food. Given a free mind, the two made wrong choices. (It seems that being in perfect circumstances didn't guarantee they would choose correctly.) Beautiful surroundings weren't enough. Lack of stress wasn't enough. Being with God didn't make them spiritual. They both disobeyed and were deceptive.

How many of us feel if we could only get our house in order, if we could get the lawn mowed and the roses to bloom, if we didn't have to go to work each day, if we didn't have those children who messed things up, if our environment were only perfect, if God was walking in our backyard where we could see Him in the cool of the day, we could be spiritual. We could pray out loud; we could write psalms; we could sing like the angels.

God doesn't ask for dramas and displays; He wants simple obedience to His directions and honesty, not deception. Our circumstances may never be anywhere close to perfection, but God will create a haven of peace, a garden of rest in our hearts, when we choose His approval over the temptations of the world.

Let's not wait for that great day when we get it all together and have time for God. Let's meet Him in the garden of our heart right now and let Him restore our souls.

❧

What about you? Are you waiting for things (or yourself) to be perfect before you come to God? Are you waiting for circumstances to improve for you to have time for Him? Choose to walk in obedience and honesty in even the smallest details of life.

Sow Well?... Reap Well!

Do you sometimes feel that you are wandering in the wilderness, that God has forgotten you—if He ever knew you in the first place? God has promised that "he will never leave you nor forsake you" (Deuteronomy 31:6 NIV). Cain (Adam's son) made wrong choices and unfortunately had to reap the consequences of what he had sown—but God did not forsake him. God meets us where we are in order to teach us. (Read Genesis 4:1–15 for more of Cain and Abel's story.)

God met with Cain and Abel in the fields where animals were grazing and grain was growing. What better place to be close to God and admire His handwork than in the fields where God's gardening plan of reaping what we sow is in such clear evidence? We see that mighty oaks grow out of little acorns, and apple trees don't grow bananas. Without God there would be no explanation for how a tiny pansy seed knows it must grow up to be a pansy and not a petunia, no chance that on occasion a grain of wheat might not become an ear of corn.

Let's stop and think right now. What are we sowing? What are we putting in our minds personally? Are we reading God's Word and Christian literature? Or are we filling our minds with trivia and trash? Garbage in; garbage out. What are we planting in the hearts of our mates and close friends? Are we inserting kind and gracious words that will produce positive responses? What seeds are we placing in the fertile minds of our little ones? How embarrassing it is sometimes to hear our own words repeated back to us out of the mouths of babes. We do reap what we sow—God's principles work in people as well as in the fields.

❧

Memorize and meditate on Galatians 6:9: "And let us not grow weary while doing good, for in due season we shall reap if we do not lose heart" (NKJV). Begin today to have a "harvest mentality." Think about what you are sowing. What kind of crops are you going to reap in your children? Your marriage? Your thought life?

Ask the Holy Spirit to show you areas where you are sowing bad seed. Then choose to change your sowing so you will reap bountifully!

In Stride

Sometimes we have a relationship with another human being where we know exactly what the other one is thinking. Our daughters, Marita and Lauren, and I are "tuned in" to each other. We are of one mind; we walk together. Whenever they are with me, they can take one look at a meeting room where I am to speak and see it with my eyes. They put themselves in my position automatically because they've been close to me for so long. Neither one has to stand and say, "What would Mother want changed or moved?" They just take action as I would; they can see with my eyes. When I am speaking, they sense when I'm too hot, when the room is too stuffy, or when I need a drink of water. We have joked for years that, since they have heard my testimony hundreds of times, if I were to faint in the middle of it, either one of them could step over me and continue my life story without missing a beat. We are not just related by blood, we are close in spirit. We have not only traveled together, we have "walked" together.

God wants us to have that kind of a fellowship with Him. He wants our relationship to be deeper than just a born-again experience; He wants us to be of one mind in the spirit—not just strolling down the path to heaven but walking with Jesus.

Are we in stride with God? Or is He several steps

ahead of us? Has God already turned the corner and disappeared from sight? Walking with God is not being cheerfully chummy with Christ but being so close to Him that we lay our head on His bosom and breathe in and out to God's rhythm.

How do we get to know Christ that well? The same way we get to know anyone. By spending time with Him. When new neighbors move in, many times we make our initial judgment on their status and taste by observing their furniture as it comes out of the moving van. But we don't really know them. To get to know our neighbors we have to walk next door, introduce ourselves, and spend some time with them.

It's the same with God; we have to spend time with Him. We all want to know Him, but we don't take the time to study His Word, to feel the power of His presence, to get in stride with God. Let's get acquainted today so we can walk in tomorrow.

❧

Jesus said in Matthew 11:28–30 that His yoke is easy and His burden is light and that He will give us rest. Don't you want to be "in stride" with the One whose yoke is easy and burden is light? (Not many friends like that around these days!) Decide today that you will spend time with the Father God and truly get to know Him.

Soggy but Saved

One summer evening Elaine was scheduled to share her testimony at a friend's poolside supper party. As the guests arrived the skies parted and rain poured onto the patio. Tables and chairs were quickly dragged into the small living room, which was so filled with furniture that there was no room for the people.

The resourceful hostess, seeing no change in the weather, decided to move the party and Elaine's performance to the garage. "This was no finished room," Elaine explained wide-eyed. "It was just a dirty old garage with a wheel-less Dodge up on jacks. Water was pouring in under the doors and piling up against the far wall. It began to look like an oil-laden swamp."

Elaine stood at a podium that was placed over the drain in the garage floor and told her life story to a sad-looking group who well may have wondered what they were doing listening to Bible verses in a garage with water swirling around their feet.

At the conclusion, the hostess, seemingly oblivious to the dampened spirits and wet shoes, asked all the guests to take off their limp name tags and add an X if they had asked the Lord into their lives. After the guests "swam" out to their cars, Elaine was too embarrassed to look at the tags, but the hostess counted the decisions and found that because Elaine had been obedient in a bizarre set of circumstances, twelve searching people found God in a garage in the rain. Never limit God by assuming certain circumstances preclude His work.

❧

Ask God to remove any preconceived ideas of how He is going to use you for glory. Isaiah 11:3 (NKJV) tells us the Lord "shall not judge by the sight of His eyes, nor decide by the hearing of His ears." Elaine could have looked at the rain and the disgruntled guests and disregarded the whole meeting. However, because she was obedient, people's eternal destinies were changed that day. We, too, must be obedient by listening to the Holy Spirit, and not judging by what we see or hear.

"For My thoughts are not your thoughts, Nor are your ways My ways," says the Lord. "For as the heavens are higher than the earth, so are My ways higher than your ways, And My thoughts than your thoughts" (Isaiah 55:8–9 NKJV).

No "Babel" Building!

In my lifetime, I have seen how many godly people with good intentions become overly impressed by their own spirituality when surrounded by an adoring audience. The world is looking for a leader to follow, a god to guide them. How easy it is, when sensing the adulation of the crowd, to see oneself as a minigod and to build a little tower of Babel.

In the Bible, an early group of leaders settled in the area of Babylon about fifty miles south of today's Baghdad, and as they structured their new civilization one of their first thoughts was to build a monument to themselves to show their power and authority. This tower was not an altar to their God but to themselves (read Genesis 11:4–9 for the rest of the story). Yet just as God dealt with these Old Testament leaders with their tower of Babel, He is still sovereign and His eyesight has not dimmed.

When God observes a ministry that has shifted its attention and worship from Him to its human leaders, He can confuse their language and scatter their ministry right before our eyes. Those of us who are visible as leaders (and even those who aren't!) must keep our eyes on the Lord and not on ourselves so that we build ministries for Him and not monuments to us.

In a world of fallen leadership, let us limited creatures be reminded that we aren't God and that we don't have any special license to sin because we've given up so much for God. We must not be tempted to mount the tower and assume the power of divinity. Instead let's ask for the wisdom from above in James 3:17 . . . "But the wisdom from above is first pure, then peaceable, gentle, willing to yield, full of mercy and good fruits, without partiality and without hypocrisy."

When we walk in this wisdom, we will be blessed in our leadership.

Jesus gave us the perfect example in leadership! Read Philippians 2:1–11. Then put these following two verses into your heart and allow the Holy Spirit to humble your heart for leadership:

"Let nothing be done through selfish ambition or conceit, but in lowliness of mind let each esteem others better than himself. Let each of you look out not only for his own interests, but also for the interests of others" (Philippians 2:3–4 NKJV).

God on the Rocks

About twenty years ago when I was a newly believing Christian and just starting to give my testimony, I was asked to speak at a retreat near Mount Shasta. When I arrived, I discovered the campgrounds and cabins were extremely rustic with few amenities. Since my idea of camping out is opening the window of a Holiday Inn, I was far from delighted over the circumstances. I soon learned that my opening message was to be given outdoors, in the dark, by a campfire. It had never occurred to me that I wouldn't speak in some kind of a building with some flicker of light, but I found myself out in a field, sitting on a rock. A few bright flames, fanned by the breeze, passed flickering shadows over the faces as the campfire lit up their eyes and the moon reflected off the top of Mount Shasta. The scene had a friendly glow until the mosquitoes came out, the moon went behind some clouds, the rocks became hard, the fire died out, and the night chill crept inside our sweaters.

Some voice out of the dark introduced me, and I gave my testimony. Occasionally the moon would peek out long enough for me to see silhouettes and know there was an audience in the shadows.

At the end, I offered up a prayer of commitment, asking those who had not yet found God in a personal way to ask Jesus Christ into their lives to change them.

There was no apparent response. In the following years as I began to speak in bigger and brighter places, I forgot that humbling evening on the rocks.

Eighteen years later I was speaking at a large retreat for women in an elegant hotel when a lovely lady approached me. "Do you remember sharing your testimony at Mount Shasta State Park?" she asked. "It was that night in the dark that I prayed with you to receive Christ. I'd been looking for God, but I'd never seen Him in the light. Somehow the protection of darkness gave me courage, and I dared to ask Jesus into my life without letting anyone know." She then filled me in on the changes in her life including a successful marriage to a Christian leader. "Thank you for being willing to come to the state park and speak. Your obedience to God changed the direction of my life."

How unworthy of her praise I felt as I remembered my attitude that night, for while I had felt a surge of self-pity for my situation, she had found God on the rocks.

❧

God's Word is powerful and brings light in the darkest of places—even to a literally dark campout on Mount Shasta. Psalm 119:130 says, "The entrance of Your words gives light; it gives understanding to the simple" (NKJV). Don't forget to be simple—simply obedient. And remember that God's ways are not complicated, and Jesus is the Rock.

Break the Chains

In the Bible, Joseph is a classic example of rising above bad circumstances. With all the problems Joseph had as a teenager (being hated by his brothers, sold into slavery, falsely accused of trying to take advantage of Potiphar's wife and thus thrown into prison . . . Read Genesis 37 through Genesis 47 for the full story), it is a miracle he grew up to be a balanced and godly man. Before you walk on toward God, check your past. Were you rejected, molested, unloved, or deprived as a child? Do you have some emotional weights of the past that you need to shed? Seek out a trusted friend or counselor and begin to deal with these past pains. For additional help read my book *Lives on the Mend,* Jan Frank's *Door of Hope,* or David Seamands's *Healing of Memories.*

Chances are you haven't been in jail, yet you may be a prisoner in some other set of circumstances. You may be locked in an alcoholic home, you may be suffering in a difficult marriage, you may be serving time for some emotional pains of the past. Many of us are in the chains and fetters of financial burdens that keep us from enjoying the freedom the Lord promises.

When Joseph went to prison for a crime he did not commit, what did he do? He didn't run and hide. He didn't deny he was there and sink into a false world of unreality. And he didn't wallow in self-pity. Instead, he faced the facts, undeserved as they were, and refused to waste energy on hatred and bitterness. He thanked God that He was alive and developed a plan of how to make the best of an unexpected tragedy. Here was an innocent man persecuted for his exemplary behavior.

Does his situation sound at all like yours? Not all punishment is deserved, and those of us who are victimized in any way have to make a decision whether to sit and cry, hating those who have done us wrong, or formulate the best possible plan, praise God, and move on. We can either focus on the prison bars over the windows or on the sky beyond.

Are you in a prison today? Is some guard trying to whip you into shape? Take a realistic view of your options, decide if you need some counsel, and move a few steps toward the door. Practice the presence of God whether in prison or in power. The truth will set you free.

&

Then you will know the truth, and the truth will set you free" (John 8:32 NIV). Don't be afraid to face the truth in your life—in doing so, the Father will set you free from your bondage.

Believing without Seeing

How many of us feel if we could only touch God, if we could witness a miracle, if we could see Him part the Red Sea, if we could observe some tangible sign of His presence, *then* we would believe?

We live in a society that doesn't want to believe in anything it can't touch, eat, possess, drive, or enjoy. We are realists; what you see is what you get. We're afraid to trust people, so we don't dare have faith in God. Yet the Bible tells us "without faith it is impossible to please God, because anyone who comes to him must believe that he exists and that he rewards those who earnestly seek him" (Hebrews 11:6 NIV).

"What is faith? It is the confident assurance that something we want is going to happen. It is the certainty that what we hope for is waiting for us, even though we cannot see it up ahead" (Hebrews 11:1 TLB).

"Faith is the substance of things hoped for, the evidence of things not seen" (Hebrews 11:1).

How do we get faith?

"Faith cometh by hearing, and hearing by the word of God" (Romans 10:17).

For us who haven't seen the parting of the Red Sea, we gain faith by studying the Word of God and reliving the times of the Old Testament heroes. The Hebrews had only to listen and obey. They had evidence of things we have not seen.

Sure we would have loved to see the parting of the Red Sea, but John 20:29 says, "Jesus said to him, 'Thomas, because you have seen Me, you have believed. Blessed are those who have *not* seen and yet have believed'" (NKJV, emphasis added). I believe Jesus is talking about us in that verse! We may have not tangibly seen our Lord, yet we believe and trust in Him, and we will be blessed as we do so!

Have you allowed yourself to get caught in the trap of having to "see to believe"? Ask the Father to forgive your unbelief and welcome the Holy Spirit to instruct you as you read God's Word and listen to His Word being taught and preached. As God's Word goes into your heart, hope will spring up (earnestly expecting God to do something good) and your faith will bloom.

Miracle on the Mountain

In November 1970, the Big Bear Burn raged through our hills. We looked up transfixed as a wild wall of flames crested our hills and marched down the mountains toward our home. Hurricane winds propelled the lighted tumbleweeds like flaming balls, and the olive trees burst like fireworks as each little, oil-laden leaf became a minitorch against a blackened sky.

My son Fred, six years old at the time, called the family to prayer as the firemen stood with hoses poised surrounding the house. He handed me a Bible and said, "Mother, read us something that will tell us God won't let our house burn." Was God with us on the mountain that night? Was He awake and not slumbering? Would He save our home if we looked to the hills?

God did deliver us from the forest fire flaming furiously around our home. When the inferno hit our deck, the winds shifted. Half the fire went on one side of us, and half went over the house and down the other side of the hill. It was our passover. It was God parting our Red Sea. It was Moses holding up his rod for a miracle to take place. We met God face to face on our mountain that night, and He has preserved our "going out" and our "coming in" ever since.

He even brought several neighbors to Himself that night, and one teenager prayed to receive the Lord while holding a hose on our roof.

When our fire had passed over us, we found one charred post that God had left as a reminder of the reality of the flames, lest we might forget. Later I hung a little plaque at the front door for each visitor to read and for me to see each day. It was that verse I'd loved as a child, but with new meaning for me and my family.

Don't wait until the fire comes before you look for God. He's on the mountain waiting for you right now.

"I will lift up mine eyes unto the hills, from whence cometh my help. My help cometh from the LORD, which made heaven and earth" (Psalm 121:1–2).

Broken Vases

One summer when I was speaking at the Bible Conference in Lake Okaboji, Iowa, an elderly and sprightly gentleman gave the evening message on the Ten Commandments. On a table before him were ten tall vases of different shapes and colors. He explained these would represent the Ten Commandments as he taught them. He then told the story of a person who knew what he should do in life but didn't. When he got to the first violation, the little man picked up a huge mallet and whacked the first vase with every ounce of strength he had. The thing smashed instantly, and pieces flew out into the audience. Everyone screamed in surprise. Had there been any dozing souls in the audience, there weren't any more. Each person was sitting up straight and alert, awaiting the other nine commandments. As he said, "And he broke the third commandment," he broke the third vase, and the audience ducked and covered their faces. There may have been better speakers that summer, but I can't remember them. I will never be able to forget the man with the mallet merrily breaking the Ten Commandments.

When he was finished, a pastor next to me told me this same gentleman had spoken at his church. In the morning service he had asked the ladies of the church to bring vases he could use in his evening message. He obviously had not communicated what he was going to do with the vases because in true female style, they all brought lovely items worthy of display in front of the entire congregation as representative pieces from their families. You can imagine the response as the man raised his mallet and smashed the first vase. The pastor said nine ladies rose from their seats, ran up the aisle, and grabbed their vases off the table while the first lady sobbed out loud. The whole program stopped, and the group sang hymns while the elders searched the church basement for old vases knowing that the show must go on. I'm sure no one in that church will ever forget the breaking of the Ten Commandments.

How about you? Is there anything about these commandments that has stayed in your mind over the years?

In our present society, we have rebelled against any restrictions, and we have cried out for our rights. We want to be free and "do our own thing." For God to give us rules seems old-fashioned—something that we had to obey as children, but now that we are mature, we can behave as we wish; we can enjoy the "good life."

We tend to feel these rules don't relate much to us today. We've rebelled against His law, and we haven't examined His precepts with an open mind.

✤

Let's look for God in His commandments, listen to what He has to say, and try not to break the vases! Study them in Exodus 20:3–17.

"I Want Your Curtains!"

Many of us can breeze through the first nine commandments (of the Ten Commandments in Exodus 20:3–17) without much difficulty. However, when you get to the tenth commandment, "Don't covet" (Exodus 20:17), you may have a problem. We are told not to desire, long for, or crave something (anything) that belongs to someone else. When I first read this commandment with meaning, I realized I coveted everything I saw. I wanted it all. Coming from a childhood without curtains or even a scatter rug, I longed for drapes and carpeting. I could rationalize that I deserved them, especially if *you* had them. Even though I know better today and I realize that greed is a form of idol worship, if I come to visit you and you have new monogrammed towels, I'll want them.

God knew where to catch us when He told us not to be envious of other people's houses and possessions. He told us not to wish we were married to the man next door, for the grass is always greener, but there may be no roots. We are not even to be grabby for the cleaning lady or the boy who cuts our neighbors' lawn, or for their poodle or Siamese cat, or for their Mazda or Mercedes, or for anything that belongs to our neighbors. Nor are we to want that position in the church that your friend acquired. (Ouch!)

Coveting is such a subtle sin that most of us don't

confess it or even dignify it with a plea for forgiveness; yet wishing we had more than we have (sometimes misnamed goal-setting, especially when the desire is to possess what our neighbor has) is a sin of great significance to God.

Coveting can be detrimental to having a pure heart before God, and it will rob you of blessings. Let's choose to address it with our Father.

Is coveting a problem for you? Is it a "hidden sin" that you really hadn't even realized you were hiding? Repent of any covetousness in your heart. Ask the Holy Spirit to prick your heart any time you unconsciously slip into the old mindset of coveting and continually renew your mind in God's Word.

Bungalow One

When God called me out of "Egypt" (my old way of life), He literally sent me to the desert of San Bernardino. In retrospect, I see that if He had left me in Connecticut with my big house and prestige in the community, I might have played around on the shores of the Red Sea, dabbling in the good ol' days of Egypt (as the Israelites were tempted to do when they left Egypt for the Promised Land of Canaan). Instead, He picked us up and placed us in Bungalow One. While Arrowhead Springs was like the Garden of Eden, Bungalow One was hardly paradise. Built in the '30s as a motel, it was like a train going around a curve. Each of the five rooms had a door opening onto a patio, and to go from one end to the other you had to go outdoors and cross the cement. The ceilings were falling in, the rugs were down to the nub, and there was no kitchen. As I cooked on a hot plate on the porch, I cried out, "God, when I sang 'I'll go where You want me to go', I didn't mean Bungalow One!"

But God did mean Bungalow One, for He knew I needed to spend some time in the desert to shake the Egypt out of me. It was while living in Bungalow One that I started studying the Bible seriously, attending lectures and classes taught by evangelists and theologians, and writing Sunday school lessons. There in the desert, Fred and I created our first marriage class for a local church which led to couples' seminars and years later became our book *After Every Wedding Comes A Marriage*. When God wants to get us out of Egypt and into His tabernacle, sometimes He lets us live for a while in the desert.

Surviving a desert experience demands a realistic appraisal of ourselves, for it strips us of pretense, pulls the props out from under us, and lets us see that we can't do it on our own. We need some outside help that is bigger than we are. Whether your time in the desert is from a broken marriage, a loss of income, or living two years in Bungalow One, whatever the cause, physical or emotional, it is a humbling, perhaps humiliating series of events that can either make you bitter for life or cause you to reach for a God who is real.

So if you're in the desert today, rejoice; the spring is just ahead. You will become "like streams of water in the desert and the shadow of a great rock in a thirsty land" (Isaiah 32:2 NIV).

❧

Don't for a minute think that God has forgotten you. He knows where you are and what lesson He wants you to learn. God is a good God, and He truly wants the best for you! You may be in the desert, but He's preparing a place for you right now!

A Real Man

Larry was an extremely attractive businessman who conducted seminars on success. He brought me in to one of his groups that met once a month to teach them about Personality Plus. Before I spoke, he gave the members their "word of the month." He explained they should write down the word *commitment*, read it every morning, and use it often in conversation. As they focused on this word, they would begin to understand commitment.

The next morning Larry called me and said he had to talk with me; would I go out to lunch with him and his wife? As we sat in a corner booth, Larry looked me in the eye and asked, "How do you find God?" For a moment I was stunned; I'd never been questioned quite so bluntly or quickly.

He continued, "I've always been a good person; but my wife just had a mastectomy, and while she was in the hospital and I was faced with the fact that she might die, I had nowhere to turn. I realized I didn't know God. How do you find Him?"

By then I had regained my composure, and I started with his teaching of the night before. "Remember how you told everyone to concentrate on the word *commitment?* Commitment to what?"

He hesitated and then answered, "Commitment in general." I shared with him that you find God when your commitment is specific—a general commitment is an intellectual exercise, but when you commit your life to Jesus, you will come face to face with God.

"I've been committed to good works," he replied, "but somehow when the chips are down, that's not enough."

I then explained that good works are commendable, but they don't bring you into a personal relationship with the Lord. I shared a passage from Ephesians: "For by grace [God's gift] are ye saved through faith [belief, commitment]; and that not of yourselves [not from your earnings and strivings]: it is the gift of God: not of works [no matter how impressive yours may have been], lest any man should boast [or take the credit]" (Ephesians 2:8–9).

"There's nothing wrong with good motives, but you won't find the peace of God until your commitment is to Jesus. You have to give up your own will and present yourself as a living sacrifice to the Lord."

I had to assure Larry that a commitment to Jesus was not a weak thing to do, but that it took a strong man to recognize he needed a power beyond himself. Larry was looking for success in life in a word; that day he found meaning to life in THE WORD of God.

※

Are you trying to be a successful, good person, thinking that will fulfill your life? Only Jesus will fulfill your life. Real men need Jesus.

Out of the Dark—into the Light

After sitting at a table writing all day, I went out to the Jacuzzi at the motel to relax my right arm and back. There I met a pleasant Canadian couple, Carl and Sue, who were on vacation, and we began to talk. When they asked what I was doing, I explained I wrote Christian books and I needed a short break from my work. Carl replied, "I'm a Christian, but just recently I met God on a new level." He then told me of a dream he had where he'd been walking down a road at dusk. Lights began to come on, and he could see the city straight ahead. As he trudged along, the stars began to shine and the moon came over a mountain.

Suddenly, everything went black, and he was alone in the dark. Flames licked up around his feet for a fleeting moment, and then they died away. There was no light, no stars, no moon, no shadows, no people, no sound. He screamed for help, and there was no response; he demanded light, but the answer was darkness. Soon he realized he was in hell.

"Where are the flames?" he called out. "I thought hell was full of fire." There was no answer, only total darkness, an utter absence of any tiny ray of light.

Then he cried out to God, "Father forgive me; I'll do anything You say if You'll take me out of the darkness into the light. Show me light; give me hope."

As Carl repeated this to me, he said he had awakened

crying, and for the first time he realized what God's Word meant when it said, "The Lord is my light and my salvation—whom shall I fear?" (Psalm 27:1 NIV). He realized that the absence of light is an affliction of the Lord, a groping in the dark, the way of the wicked (Deuteronomy 28:28–29 NIV).

As we discussed darkness in the hot California sun, Carl concluded, "I've believed in God forever, but I hadn't fully understood the necessity of Jesus saying, 'I am the light of the world. Whoever follows me will never walk in darkness, but will have the light of life'" (John 8:12 NIV).

Carl groped for God in a dream of darkness and found Him in a new light.

❧

Ask the Lord to give you a fresh revelation that Jesus is the light of the world. Think about lost relatives and friends that literally are "groping in darkness" and need the light of Jesus. Ask the Holy Spirit to bring to mind those you need to lift up in prayer today.

Dare to Dream . . .
Get Off the Porch Swing!

Many of us feel that we haven't "made it" in life, or for that matter, we weren't "made" for dreaming big. Some of us may say, "I wish I had a sense of humor. I can't sing or act or think up clever things.

Some of us may have had parents who thought we didn't amount to "a hill of beans." Some of us may have little education or a feeling that we're not smart enough to become anything.

A few of us may have achieved great goals or made a lot of money, but we still feel insecure inside. Perhaps we've asked ourselves, "Who am I?" and not heard a clear answer.

No matter where we are in our self-evaluation today, we can move on. We can *dare to dream.*

It's always easier to relax than reach, to give up than grasp, but we want to stretch rather than just settle into the status quo. If we rested until the perfect path to success opened before us, we would all be sitting on the porch swing of life waiting for directions. Let's pretend that's where we are today, all of us lined up on that glider on the veranda looking out to blue skies and sunshine forever. We can smell the sweet flowers of success, but if we're going to pick them we'll have to get up. We can see ideas flitting around like hummingbirds, but to use one we'll have to get a net and capture it. Some of us would prefer to rock where we are than to get up and move on. Some prefer to accept what's good rather than to aim for the best. Some would rather sit on a safe swing than to *dare to dream*.

Proverbs 29:18 tells us, "Where there is no vision, the people perish," and yet many of us are without a vision taking the fatalistic approach that "if God wanted me to have a better job He'd send a personnel manager to my front porch."

Don't be a porch-swing person any longer. Don't stuff your laurels into a pillow and rest upon them. Don't rock in indecision and inertia.

I'm calling you off the porch. God has great plans for you! Come on, let's head for the starting gate.

※

Are you willing to dare to dream? Or is fear of failure or rejection keeping you in the porch swing? Ask the Father to give you His vision for your life. You were created for a particular purpose! Go ahead and dream and ask God to direct you. Remember, many great visions start with small dreams!

Purple Hair

All of us are born with natural creativity and with inquisitive minds. Each little child pictures his own brand of Santa Claus, guardian angels, and the tooth fairy. When asked to draw a view of God, each child has his own personal creation. If we started out wide-eyed and inventive, when did it stop? Who cut it off? Who put our ideas into a little box and said, "This is the norm. This is the way we think around here."

I remember when my daughter Marita's teacher called me in to discuss why Marita drew a picture of me with purple hair. The teacher, searching for some psychological truth, had told Marita to make my hair a "normal color." When I asked Marita why she had given me purple hair, she said simply, "They didn't have any blonde crayons." Marita's type of creativity wasn't acceptable to her teacher.

We've all heard the expression, "He burst my bubble." It's sometimes used to excuse why we didn't pursue a certain dream or why we lost our initial enthusiasm for some project. But often our bubble is burst because our type of creativity wasn't "acceptable" and someone wiped out our desire.

I meet many people who tell me sadly that they have no creativity (usually because their desire or creativity was wiped out by someone along the way). By that they mean they're not artists or opera singers. Few of us are, and yet we are all born with a God-given ability to think creatively.

God had a purpose, and then He created you specifically for that particular purpose. He put *all* the *creativity* that you needed in you to be able to fulfill that particular purpose. Yet you must choose to release that creativity in your life and realize that your creativity will be different from any other person's on earth.

That's how *creative* God is—He made each one of us completely unique and designed each of us to fulfill a particular destiny!

❦

Have you ever stopped to ponder the magnitude of God's creativity? Wow! From the galaxies to each intricate human life—God is creativity! And when we have asked Jesus into our lives as Lord and Savior, our creative Father God dwells within us! Ask the Holy Spirit to release the spirit of creativity in your life today.

Bubbles in the Bathtub

Picture for a moment a bathtub. It's empty, cold, and hard. Now turn on the faucet and adjust it to the perfect temperature for you. Something cold is warming up. Now pour in some bubble bath, and suddenly the ordinary becomes exciting. The aroma is pleasant, but the best part is watching the bubbles grow. Out of one tablespoon of liquid comes a mountain of bubbles. So little becomes much. The stronger the force of the water, the bigger the bubbles become. Is there anyone of us who can resist the temptation of jumping into such pleasure? Some of you may want to go right now and start running the water, throw in some bath beads, hop in, and continue to read.

But what happens if you get called to the phone before you get in the tub? You shut off the faucet and leave the warm bubbles that may have mounded even higher than the tub itself, intending to come right back. However, the cares of the world detain you, and when you return, the fluff and the fun have gone out of the bubbles. They've died down a bit, and many have disappeared forever. But all is not lost. You turn on the water again full force, and with the new encouragement fresh bubbles appear. The water gets warm again. You've revived what seemed to be dying.

Now consider our childhood minds. We've each been given at least a capful of creativity. Left in the bottle it doesn't produce any new ideas, but poured out into a warm environment it begins to bubble. The stronger the encouragement, the fuller the force, the more bubbles appear. So many little children are just bubbling over with enthusiasm and excitement, their minds overflowing with creative thoughts. But what happens if we get left alone with no one stirring up the waters, no one keeping the bubbles alive? After a while the enthusiasm cools down. The bubbles burst and we're left with just a tub of cold water and perhaps the remnant of a few tiny bubbles here and there. But don't despair. We can turn on the tap again. We can bring some of the bubbles back to life. They won't be as big or as lively, but they can be stirred up one more time.

❧

Think about your creativity as a child. Was it heated up and encouraged? When you poured yourself out, were you allowed to bubble to the surface? Or were you left alone with no one fluffing up your bubbles until one by one they popped and disappeared? What about your children's creativity? Do you "burst their bubbles"? What about your mate's? Be encouraged today to dream with creativity—and let's put the "bubbles" back into our lives!

The Listening Challenge

In my early years of marriage, I felt that God personally anointed me with a gift for filling in gaps in potentially boring conversations. My children noticed my talent as they were growing up and created their own biblical paraphrase, "Where two or three are gathered together, Mother will give a seminar." One day I heard Lauren explain to a friend after I had entertained them with a dramatic delivery of a familiar family fable, "That is the fifth time I've heard that story, and each time it has a different ending."

Some fainthearted mothers might have taken this as an insult, but I chose to consider it as a testimony to my creativity. Didn't Lauren's friends agree that I was the most fun mother on Beechwood Drive? Wasn't I the only mother who had memorized the entire Dr. Seuss book *Green Eggs and Ham* and was willing to recite it at the drop of a *Cat in the Hat*? At the conclusion of my recitation where Sam-I-Am has tasted green eggs and ham and likes them, I would review the moral of the story that we should all try at least a little bit of each item offered. Then I would send the children home to eat their dinners with a new sense of surprise and anticipation.

One day Fred came up with a statement worthy of Socrates and those other sages: "Do you realize that when you are talking, you're not learning anything because what you're saying you already know?" I had to admit I'd never thought of that heavy homily before. He went on to lovingly point out that he felt I had come to a place in life where I should pay attention to what other people were saying. "You might even learn something," he concluded. I agreed to take up his challenge.

Fred's lesson fifteen years ago was a turning point. I began to develop questions to ask on a deeper level than "What's your name?" and "Where do you live?" As I began to write books, I found that every person I met had a story inside waiting for someone to set it free. In fact, I've been able to continue writing each year because I've learned to listen. I understand why God gave us two ears and only one mouth!

⁂

It takes a lot more character to be a good listener than it does to be a good talker. Take inventory on your listening skills. Do you interrupt others before they are finished? Do you finish their sentences for them? Ask the Holy Spirit to help you truly listen to others.

Is Your Life an Act?

As I finished giving my life story at a church service in Auckland, New Zealand, a lady said to me, "I can't believe how honest you are. We aren't used to that here. We always cover up how we really feel."

A man in California stated, "You and Fred are the first honest Christian speakers we've ever heard."

A lady in Texas approached me in tears, "I cried through much of your message. It wasn't that it was sad, but that it made me feel some emotion that I'd kept stuffed inside for years."

These comments represent hundreds of people who have shared with us that they are surprised and often touched by our willingness to be honest and transparent before others. It's a sad commentary on current relationships that transparency is rare and cover-up is the norm. We are constantly amazed that honesty is so unusual it deserves comment.

We seem to be acting in some gigantic play. We get up in the morning and tell ourselves who we are today. We put on our makeup and our plastic smile. We add a look of determination and power. We practice our lines on the way to work, and we try not to show displeasure when the rest of the cast feeds us the wrong lines. We push down any inappropriate feelings, keep our masks in place, dance to the beat of the daily drummer, and exit exhausted. No wonder! It's difficult and draining to play a role each day and not step out of character. Yet that's where we find so many people—working to be who they aren't, afraid to utter a real thought.

People are afraid to be real because they don't want to make themselves vulnerable. So many of us have been wounded by rejection that we have erected gigantic walls to keep the world out. Obviously huge walls are not very transparent!

We can come to a place of transparency and vulnerability only when we truly know who we are in Christ—we are children of the King! When we understand that we are affirmed in Christ, accepted and loved in spite of anything we may have done or not done (Ephesians 1:6), we won't be constantly needing the approval of man. God's approval will be sufficient, and we no longer will fear man's rejection.

Do you have walls built up around you? Are you walking in fear of being rejected? Ask the Father to affirm you as His child and dismantle the root of rejection in your life. Tear down the walls and be free to be the real you!

Memorize Romans 8:15–16: "For you did not receive the spirit of bondage again to fear, but you received the Spirit of adoption by whom we cry out, 'Abba, Father.' The Spirit Himself bears witness with our spirit that we are children of God" (NKJV).

The Author

From the time I was a child I loved being on the stage. I memorized little poems to recite in the church talent shows and tried out for every local play. In high school I won poetry-reading contests, starred in plays, and was on the debate team. As a speech teacher, I directed high school shows, started a drama club, and made my wedding into a theatrical production. Later I directed musical comedies and was on the founding staff of the Long Wharf Theatre in New Haven, Connecticut. Throughout all these years I loved anything connected with theatricals.

What I did not realize at the time was that my whole life had become an act. Fred and I played roles at home as well as on stage; we each portrayed the picture of a perfect parent. We lived on the right side of the tracks, surrounded our children with luxuries, and dressed them in appropriate costumes. Our home became a stage set with each room having its own theme. Everything had to be kept in perfect order so that if anyone came to the front door I could give them a house tour with full confidence.

It was in the midst of what we now call "Mother's Stage Phase" that my musical comedies turned into tragedy. My two little sons were diagnosed with a fatal brain disease, and there was nothing any of us could do about it. There was no happy ending for the Littauer show.

As I look back, I can see that God used our tragic circumstances to get my attention and get me off the stage where I was starring in my own show. He humbled me as He took my hand and led me from my twelve-room Connecticut home into shabby, old Bungalow One which was falling in around me.

We plastered the holes in the ceilings, replaced the dripping "swamp coolers" with air conditioners, and made the porch into a kitchen. We had a new *setting* for our new life.

We studied God's Word, listened to every visiting lecturer, and began to teach an adult Sunday school class called "Harmony in the Home." We had a new *script.*

We instituted a daily prayer time, had family meetings, and began to raise Christians instead of just children. We had a whole new *theme.*

We searched the Scriptures for information on parenting, called to God for direction in discipline, and concentrated on building a Christian home. We had a new *plot,* God's plan for our life.

Most important of all, we recognized that we had a new *Author,* a Lord who knew the beginning from the end, the alpha from the omega, because He had written both the words and the music.

Jesus is *"the author and finisher of our faith"* (Hebrews 12:2).

A Quiet Sabotage

How do we pursue unity? First, let's start with our differences because our aim is not to obliterate our own personalities but to understand our differences and accept the other person as he or she is, not try to change each other. I teach this to you not as an academic exercise but from the heart of a mother and a wife of thirty-five years who has lived it both ways. For fifteen years of our marriage Fred did his best to shape me up. After a while my resistance to constant training became so strong that I worked at quiet sabotage. Since open rebellion didn't go over well with Fred, I just plotted to undermine what he planned so perfectly. I became the popular mother, the fun one. "Come to me, and you will live abundantly."

When Fred was on business trips I would say, "The ogre's gone; now we can have a good time. We can all stay up late, eat when we feel like it, and not bother checking off our work charts." We would live it up and have what we called "a high old time."

The night before Fred returned I'd line the children up at the charts, check off the whole week's work, and let them know the fun was about over. The minute Fred arrived he would go immediately to the charts to make sure we had been functioning properly while he was away. We would all beam proudly and try to look like dutiful angels as he observed our obedience.

I look back on the act now and am appalled at how Fred and I were running this show with two sets of directions, not even realizing what we were doing or how harmful it was to the children to live with such parental instability. When we became committed believers we didn't change overnight, but the Lord began to peel back our self-protective layers, and we saw that we were leading the same army in two different directions. As soon as we saw the need for unified instructions, we began searching God's Word for family verses. Through God's Word and His grace we became unified as parents and as a family. We changed, and so can you. There is hope. As you pursue this change, God will bring your marriage and family into unity.

❧

If we confess our sins, he is faithful and just and will forgive us our sins and purify us from all unrighteousness" (1 John 1:9 NIV).

Enlist the Troops!

Are you stressed out trying to do all that you have to do and still have time to relax with your mate and children? Part of our problem is not allowing all the family "team" to be involved. We need to train our children in the area of home responsibilities. This will help them get along without us later in life.

Our children must learn at a very young age that there is no great housekeeping angel who swoops down and does dishes. There are no nocturnal elves who scamper through the house wielding feather dusters. We are those elves and angels, and we must do the work. It is always easier for mother angel to do it all herself, but the time spent in training the troops will be well worth the trouble in the long run.

Our family work chart had the children's names as well as Fred's and mine. If I noticed something broken, I would write it in Fred's column and if the children had a need they could write a request in mine.

We started our chart with Saturday because that was our big workday at home, and we left a big space for me to fill in. On Thursday evening I wrote out the duties for Saturday and some for the following week.

Our rule, agreed upon at the family meeting was that you could do your chores any time from Friday on, but you couldn't leave the house on Saturday until they were completed, inspected, and crossed off. This led to midnight cleaning binges and early morning vacuuming, but I always let them know I didn't care when they did the work or even who did it. If they wished to trade off, import friends, or hire a cleaning lady, I didn't mind as long as they got the job done.

I remember waking up around midnight one Friday and hearing voices in Marita's bathroom. I got up and went in to find a little blonde girl scrubbing the toilet. When I asked her what she was doing there, she replied that they were all going to the beach early the next day and Marita couldn't go with them until her chores were done and so they'd come over to help her. "They" were three of Marita's friends all in their early teens who had sneaked out of their own homes to come over and clean mine. Only a popular Sanguine (the fun-loving temperament) could inspire her friends to run away from home in the night in order to clean someone else's toilet!

Our children grew up with a good sense of responsibility and they all have a balanced view of home responsibility. So, if you've been waiting to "enlist your troops," go ahead. It's worth it!

❦

Remember that training up each child in the way he should go is not just to make your workload easier, but to prepare him to become a responsible adult who will be able to get along without you.

Letting a House Be a Home

While I have always designed the type of home that could be a showplace, Fred and I had to learn to give up some perfectionism in exchange for personalization—little touches like Freddie's scribble painting hanging on the refrigerator door and Marita's clay pinch pot proudly placed on the coffee table. I had to hold myself back from correction when the napkins they chose in setting the table were not the "best choice." And I had to allow Sanguine Marita the freedom to rearrange her furniture every other week.

We need to communicate to our family members that their desires are more important than impressing our friends with a perfect house.

One time when I was speaking on parenting in Texas, I mentioned the idea of decorating our home for our family, not our friends. I asked the audience, "Why do we want our houses to be perfect? Whom do we decorate for?" They sheepishly answered "our friends." Are you guilty of that? We need to realize that our friends will come and go; we'll move on or they'll move on, but our families are with us forever. Our aim needs to be to create a setting where our family is comfortable, a place where they'll want to be. A lady came up to me after the seminar and said, "My husband says my house is so perfect he doesn't dare sit down. I'm going home and mess it up a little so my family can relax."

Is your house a "home"? Have you done more than move in? Do you realize the value of setting a pleasant, warm, relaxing backdrop for your family drama? Do you comprehend the value of having your children want to be home? Are you building a foundation that will provide security for your family structure and an example for your children's future homes?

Our aim is to provide a loving atmosphere, a colorful backdrop for our cast of characters to enjoy—a setting of compassion and comfort, of love and laughter. That is the setting where a house is a home. And in a home, our families are free to learn and grow in the Lord.

❧

Sometimes it is good to look at things in a simple and practical manner. Making our homes a place of joy and refuge is so important. We live in such a chaotic world that going home needs to be something that we and our children look forward to every day. Ask the Father to even help you in the simple details in making your house a home.

He Said, "I Love You"

We all know that our children grow up reflecting what they have seen in us, for we serve as daily examples. If we desire our children to pray and believe in God, we must make sure they see those traits in us.

My friend, Mike Wagner told me he had disciplined his four-year-old Joshua by explaining what he had done wrong and then telling him, "You, Joshua, have to learn to obey your parents when you are small so that when you become older and Jesus talks to you, you will know to listen to Him and obey Him."

It is never too early to train a child to hear God's voice. As we make prayer a part of everyday life, we show our children that prayer is a normal function like eating and not a boring religious ritual.

Jan and Don Frank experienced a precious example of reaping the joy of watching their children grow and understand prayer. They have used much of their family time to instill Christian principles into their little girls' lives and to teach them Bible verses and hymns. Recently they instituted a new method of prayer for the family. They all sat on the floor and prayed that God would speak to each one of them. After a period of silence Don closed in prayer and noticed tears in Heather's eyes. He asked what was wrong and the little six-year-old child replied, "You didn't give God enough time to talk to me."

At bedtime Jan sat down with Heather on the side of her bed and prayed again that God would speak to her. They waited quietly and after a while Heather lifted her head with a smile.

"Did God speak to you?" Jan asked.

"Yes," Heather said softly.

"What did He say?"

"He said, 'I love you.'"

What a lesson for a little child to be helped by her parents to hear the voice of God and know God loves her.

When we are His, we can hear His voice.

❦

We can see the importance of training our children to listen and know God's voice. But how about you? Do you "give God time to speak to you"? Or do you do all the talking when you pray? Decide today that you will give God time to talk to you. He wants to tell you He loves you too.

Even if "Your" Parents Didn't

As I talk with people who have problems with their children rebelling and ask how they have demonstrated their love, the frequent answer is something like, "My parent never kissed me and I lived." So there! Recently I talked with the preteen children of a pastor who frequently spoke of God's love from the pulpit, but they were convinced he didn't love them at all. "He never puts his arm around us or says a kind word. He's all business at home and is happiest when we stay out of sight."

As I talked with the father about the family's craving for affection, he dismissed their needs as immaturity and a lack of spirituality. "My father didn't waste any time with physical affection. Why should I?"

Obviously, if we were all perfect and ready to ascend, we would be so in tune with the Lord that His love would transcend any human need for attention. But since we as parents aren't yet on the lofty level, we can't expect our children to be that spiritually mature. When the parent does not express a warm, caring, touching love, the children either shut down their emotions or go out looking for love in all the wrong places.

If your parents didn't give this kind of affection to you, break this negative pattern. Don't be proud of it. One wife said, "I've sent the children to run and jump on their father when he comes home at night, and to tell him they love him. But he never responds. They could as well be hugging a post. He's just like his father."

We don't have to be like our fathers. We can determine today to open our hearts and begin to love our children no matter what our parents were like. The Lord will give us a new love when we ask, because it is His will that we establish a positive environment in which to raise Christians, not just children.

Why not start tonight with a Children's Hour, a time when you put aside all else, have a pause in the day's occupation, and put your eyes upon the emotional needs of your family? If you win the world and lose your children, what have you really gained?

"Not Now, Later"

Each busy day is followed by another one, and if we wait until life smoothes out before we spend time with our children, it may be too late. We may get to that last syllable of recorded time and find we never had any.

I remember Lauren looking up at me one day as I rushed about doing great and wonderful things and saying, "I know what should be engraved on your tombstone."

I wasn't planning on dying right away, but out of curiosity I asked what she had in mind. She replied, "Not now, later." I didn't know how to respond because I realized I did say that frequently. She tried different ways to communicate her feelings that I was always too busy "right now" but "some other time" would soon be along. I had good intentions, just "Not now, later." The thought of being dead and gone with Lauren's remembrance of me being "Not now, later," did catch my attention.

Ask your children what they'd put on your tombstone. You might be surprised.

If some of us parents look at time away from our children as our moment of relief, if some of us withdraw bedtime stories as discipline, if some of us won't give our children what we didn't get, and if many of us mean to be good parents some other time, what can we do about it?

Realize parenting is a God-given assignment. "A child left to himself bringeth his mother to shame" (Proverbs 29:15). Our duty is to care for our children and spend time with them. "Children are an heritage of the LORD: and the fruit of the womb is his reward" (Psalm 127:3). There is no greater reward than seeing your children as grown-up, well-adjusted Christian believers and knowing that the Lord is saying, "Well done, good and faithful father and mother. Well done." But this end product doesn't just happen; it takes purposeful planning.

We must plan to take time now, not later, for our children. Our children must become our priority over our "busy-ness." We have to correct the wrong perspective of the world's mentality that children can "fend for themselves." Our children need us to love them and spend time with them. The Father God trusted us enough, as their parents, to give them to us to train for Him. What a privilege.

❧

Do your children feel that they are "in the way" or "extra work"? Of course you love them and want to spend time with them, but what is keeping you from actually doing it? Are you too busy with "important things"? Ask the Father to help you put things in the right perspective—the season your children will be living with you is so very short. Don't miss the blessing.

Manners Memory

Would you be embarrassed if you brought your child to my home and when I placed a meal before him he said, "What is that? I don't like that!"? I've had little guests who made such comments, and while it hasn't ruined my evening, it has humiliated the parents. How can you prevent such events? The patterns have to be established at home if you want them in public. So it's an important part of parenting, especially for Christians, because the world is watching!

Probably because Fred was in the restaurant business when we married, he placed a high value on interesting meals and manners—thus he trained me to be a gourmet cook. Our children always had to try every-thing. They didn't have to like it or eat all of it, but they had to have three bites. By insisting they try each new item, we were able to train them to be adventurous eaters, and both girls are gourmet cooks. I never had to worry that they would refuse to eat at someone's house or that they would make negative comments.

One night we were out for dinner at a friend's house and we were each served a plate of escargots that looked remarkably like what we had been killing along our front walk with snail pellets. I had never served any such items, and I looked toward Marita and Fred Jr. Both of them had terror in their eyes, but they made no comment.

We all watched the host, as we had trained them to do, and followed his pattern. Sticking the little fork inside the shell wasn't difficult, but the little plop the snail made as he was pulled out almost undid us all. Marita swallowed hers whole followed by water, and Fred put bread in his mouth and chewed the little creature up with the bread.

When we left the home Fred and I praised them for the noble efforts and we proclaimed them to be gourmet eaters. As in any lesson we can't teach our children what we refuse to do. Try broadening your culinary horizons at home and train your children to take a few bites of everything without comment.

One of the most disheartening responses for me to receive from a guest after I have prepared a meal is, "Don't bother to serve the children any of that; they won't eat it." I've been amazed at how often, if I get these same children alone in the kitchen, I can encourage them to try something they've never had and enjoy it.

Teach them and yourselves to try it. You might like it.

Our children are going to be the "cream of the crop" in the next generation. Our children need to set the examples in every area of life for the lost world. Even manners are important, and what our children see us do, they will do. Take the time to train your children in excellence—others will notice the difference.

Judge Myself?

How can we begin the process of growing up? Paul tells us that our first job is to look at ourselves, sit back objectively, and see if we ever outgrew our childhood. In Galatians 6:4 he says clearly, "Let each one examine his own work" (NKJV).

"But Paul, it's so easy for me to see what's wrong with others. I have such talent in this direction."

And it was true. After fifteen years of living with Fred, I had a list of his immature manifestations that would have convicted him in any court. I even had professional proof, as my obstetrician had once told me my marriage problems stemmed from Fred's immaturity. How happy I would have been to tell Fred he was behaving like a child! However, Paul did not say I should judge Fred, but myself.

"You mean, dear Paul, there might be something wrong with *me*?"

In 1 Corinthians 11:28 Paul answered, "A man ought to examine himself" (NIV).

"Not Fred?"

In 2 Corinthians 13:5 Paul repeated, "Examine yourselves . . . ; test yourselves" (NIV).

As I conversed with Paul he seemed to say, "Florence, when you get to heaven, God is not going to give you a reward for how well you remade Fred but for how freely you let God remake you."

"You mean I'm part of the problem?"

"Yea, verily, even you."

What is our goal in the Christian life? If it is not to shape up others, what is it? Paul instructs us to "grow up in Christ."

Since our own human control keeps us self-centered, we only grow up when we "grow up in Christ." Paul speaks to us on this subject when he writes in Ephesians 4:13b–16, "We shall become mature people, reaching to the very height of Christ's full stature. Then we shall no longer be children. . . . We must grow up in every way to Christ, who is the head. . . . The whole body grows and builds itself up through love" (TEV).

❧

We can never grow up in Christ until we study His life and read God's Word to learn what He wants us to know. Take a step toward maturity today and read and study Ephesians 4:13–16. Let each one of us study God's Word so that we might grow up in Christ.

A Blaming Baby

How easy it is when things go wrong to blame other people!

"If only I had a different husband, I would be happy."

"If only I had more money, I could put up with him."

"If it weren't for those kids, I might get something done around here."

"If my mother had only loved me, I would know how to love my children."

"If I had had a decent boss, I wouldn't have been fired."

"If only my husband didn't drink, we could have a good marriage."

If only the other people were perfect, we would be all right! If we were surrounded by delightful people who thought exactly as we did and were excited by our every suggestion, life would be much more pleasant. Unfortunately, this utopia will never come true, and we must grow up to accept the personalities around us *as they are*.

One morning as I came out to breakfast, Freddie, who was nine at the time, walked in the door from the patio. I said, "Well, Freddie, how are things going with you this morning?" He sighed, "Pretty good so far—I haven't run into any people yet."

How much easier life would be if we didn't run into any other people! Ha! It is those other people with those other ideas that really get us upset. In any problem we must ask ourselves, "What part of this situation is my fault?" As long as we put the blame on others, we will never grow up.

Maybe blaming *others* is not your problem. Yet blaming is still a part of your life.

"It's this house that has me down."

"It's this town that's depressing."

"It's my husband's hours that ruin our fun."

"It's those cheap clothes that make me ugly."

How easy it is to blame our situation for our daily discontent! Let's stand tall and learn to take responsibility for our actions. And as we learn to walk in Christ we will *mature* in Him.

※

*D*o a self-inventory right now. Do you blame others for your unhappiness? Do you blame situations? Do you blame what you lack in life? Or do you make excuses and rationalize? Make the choice to be mature in Christ.

If Only My Mate Would . . .

One of the earliest problems in any marriage comes because we buy an attractive package without evaluating the contents, and when we get it home and live with it awhile we want to take it back for a cash refund. But there is no clearinghouse for mismatched marriages—we can't turn each other in—so we do the only other logical thing: we try to remake our new mates.

For those of you still busy with attempted reconstruction, still holding the hammer and nails, still mixing the patching plaster, I have bad news: it just won't work. Fred and I are living proof that two positive people with sincere purpose could not remake each other in fifteen long years.

We could not transform each other no matter how hard we tried. Why do we put forth such tremendous effort on such a losing cause? Because we are each born with a selfish nature, and we are determined to manipulate our circumstances until they suit our desires.

Fred and I were both self-centered, and we did not live up to the other's expectations. Is that possibly where you are today? Are you still watching for your "if onlys" to come true? Are you stuck with a Subaru when you wanted a Seville? Oh, what's a person to do?

Paul gives us perfect advice in Philippians 2:3–4: "Don't do anything from selfish ambition, or from a cheap desire to boast, but be humble toward one another, always considering others better than yourselves. And look out for each other's interests, not just for your own" (TEV). If this one verse could be prayerfully applied to each family, what great changes could take place! When Fred decided to accept me as I was and gave me approval and even admiration, I began to improve. When I stopped telling Fred how great I was and instead started to cook, he began to appreciate me. When each of us started to put the other's needs and interests first, we got the results we had been seeking for fifteen years.

How can you improve your marriage? Stop trying to change your partner, and get to work on yourself.

One night Fred and I were driving to the theater with another couple. The wife was grumbling with dissatisfaction, and the man said, "What can I do with her?" Fred answered, "Start working on yourself." The man retorted, "But there's nothing wrong with me. She's the one that's unhappy. I don't have a problem." Fred said quietly but firmly, "If you have an unhappy wife, *you have* a problem."

It is so much easier to put the blame for discord on the other person than to take action ourselves. Think about some problem in your marriage relationship and pray that the Holy Spirit will begin to help you apply the principles given in the following devotionals.

The Cure for Marriage Problems

1. Decide if you want to improve the situation.

I used to think that every woman with a problem wanted an answer. I assumed that if I threw out a solution to a man, he would snap it up and run home with it tucked under his arm, eager to put it into play. In fact, I was so sure that all troubled people would jump for my remedies that I originally wrote this lesson without this first step.

But the more I worked with real-life people with real-life problems, the more I began to see how few wanted to do something to improve their situation. I soon realized that if they couldn't grab hold of step number one and decide to take action no matter what their partner did, there was no point in bothering with the rest of the steps at all. I found I could lay out brilliant plans for a life, but if the person before me had no desire to move, the thoughts and the time were wasted. So often a person is unwilling to take the first step until he sees that his partner's change is under way. Consequently, neither one improves, and they sit in a series of stalemates. Therefore, it is imperative that we work on *ourselves* instead of our mates.

One principle the Lord has clearly taught me is that God holds *me* accountable for *my* actions, not my mate's reactions! We are responsible for *our* obedience (not theirs!).

Isaiah 1:19 says, "If ye be willing and obedient, ye shall eat the good of the land."

Are you willing to obey what God wants for your life, or are you going to resist until your partner shapes up? Are you willing to go all the way, looking for nothing in return? *Remember, God holds you accountable for your actions, not the other person's reactions.*

Memorize my favorite verse on this subject: "God is always at work in you to make you willing and able to obey his own purpose" (Philippians 2:13 TEV). Is it God's purpose that Christians have positive, happy, exemplary marriages? You bet it is! Then are you willing to do more than your part and stop trying to shape up your mate?

❧

Decide if you want to improve the situation—not gloss it over, run away from it, cover it up, or look the other way. Once you have made the decision to work on your problem regardless of your partner's attitude, you are ready for step two.

The Cure for Marriage Problems

2. Examine yourself. Take an objective look and find your own errors.

Now that you have made the decision to work on your problem regardless of your partner's attitude, you can objectively examine yourself. If we were trying to handle our problems in a strictly human manner, we would now be at a point where we would heroically try to change ourselves by our own power. Secular seminars are telling us we are little gods; we can do all things ourselves.

There is much we can do for ourselves. We women can change our hairstyles, lose ten pounds, buy new clothes, and repaint the kitchen. You men can buy new cars, grow a mustache, or have an affair with your secretary. These are all changes, but they won't make you a different person. Internal, lasting changes come from above, not from without.

Many women I counsel put all their faith in some super weekend with some pseudo-saint, only to fall apart when they fail to ascend.

Fred and I tried to improve in our own strength, but we gave up. We couldn't understand how we could be so competent in the world and yet so weak with each other.

We found the key to inner change in the Bible where Paul said, "I can do all things through Christ who strengthens me" (Philippians 4:13 NKJV).

As Fred and I committed our lives to the Lord we were able to admit our failures and ask for help—two very humbling experiences. Fred had been brought up in a cult that said there is no sin in the world, and I had always been so religious that it was close to impossible for us to agree with Paul when he said, "Christ Jesus came into the world to save sinners; of whom I am chief" (1 Timothy 1:15). Could good little me possibly be bad?

Only when we were willing to admit our faults and our inability to overcome them by our own strength were we ready for step three.

❧

Ask the Holy Spirit to guide you as you examine yourself. Take into consideration your temperament and be willing to be vulnerable before the Lord. Remember there is no condemnation for those who are in Christ Jesus (Romans 8:1) and that this is a vital step in the healing of your relationship.

The Cure for Marriage Problems

3. Confess your weaknesses as sin.

4. Ask God to rid you of this sin.

When we are willing to truly admit our faults and acknowledge that we are not capable of overcoming them in our own strength, we can confess these weaknesses to our forgiving Father God.

God tells us clearly, "If we confess our sins, he is faithful and just to forgive us our sins, and to cleanse us from all unrighteousness." He then adds (in case we don't think we've really been unrighteous), "If we say that we have not sinned, we make him a liar, and his word is not in us" (1 John 1:9–10).

Even though you may be a very good person, what is there about you that is offensive to others? Where do you need improvement? What habit have you been unable to break? What has just come into your mind? Confess this to the Lord, and He will free you from this bondage. Don't hide it any longer—bring it out into the open before the Lord, and He will give you forgiving peace.

"I acknowledged my sin unto thee, and mine iniquity have I not hid. I said, I will confess my transgressions unto the LORD; and thou forgavest the iniquity of my sin" (Psalm 32:5).

How hard it is for many of us "really good people" to confess to the Lord our hidden sins! It is possible to grow as a Christian and yet not deal with uncleansed areas of our lives, but we never have a clear conscience until we have pulled out the hidden sins and placed them before the Lord with a confessing heart. Perhaps you've left some sin in your life festering in a corner. Perhaps you've rationalized why it's not your fault at all. Perhaps you've shoved it into a closet but the stench keeps seeping out.

Maybe you have been hurt, yet your sin is that you have taken offense and built up walls around you. Don't try to keep your failures under wraps. Bring them out in the open and confess them to the Lord and ask Him to rid you of these sins. God never gossips or tells tales. You can trust the truth with Him!

❧

Maybe your sins are not blatant, but they are hidden sins—even hidden sins of the heart. What is it that you feel the Holy Spirit prodding you to confess to the Father? Take the time and allow the Holy Spirit to bring to your mind any unconfessed sin. You may want to write out your confession. You can have confidence that the Father is faithful to forgive you and rid you of anything and everything you confess to Him (1 John 1:9; 5:14–15).

The Cure for Marriage Problems

5. Forgive your partner silently and apologize orally.

Few of us enjoy forgiving others because it implies that what they did wasn't so bad, when it really was! If we really forgive we might forget the evidence, and what if we need it for proof in the future? Our minds function on such a selfish level that we don't like to let go of the bad examples of others. Not only do we not want to forgive, but we take pride in repeating the tales of others' grand mistakes because it shows we don't do any of these things ourselves. Obviously, if I have the discernment to see the error of your ways then I must be above suspicion myself.

I used to gather up Fred's faults with the fervor of a child picking berries. I had a whole shelf of overflowing baskets before the concept of forgiveness fell heavily upon me. To be spiritual, I plucked out a few of Fred's faults and forgave them, but I didn't want to clear the whole shelf. Where would I go for future reference material?

God had to hit me over the head with my own bulging baskets before I was ready to forgive and willing to apologize. Even though I have learned this lesson and taught this lesson, I still pick up a basket now and then and gather up some faults.

Why am I the only woman who married a man who doesn't come home at 5:30 for dinner? Why doesn't Fred pay our bills on the first day of the month automatically like every other husband? Why does he go into the office on Saturday to check a few things and then stay all day and think he was only gone an hour?

You see how easy it is for me to find Fred's failures? They jump right up and cling to me like lint on a blue suit. Does this sound familiar to any of you? Have you been out berry picking? Have you gathered in a bountiful harvest?

Put it all in the trash today. Get rid of all bitterness, wrath, and anger. "Be ye kind one to another, tenderhearted, forgiving one another, even as God for Christ's sake hath forgiven you" (Ephesians 4:32).

⁂

Learn the lesson of forgiveness and apologies before it is too late. The result will not only be a better relationship, but it will also take away the guilt. Humble yourself and break down the barriers in your relationship by forgiving and apologizing. You may also need to forgive yourself. Dump your baskets today!

The Cure for Marriage Problems

6. Look at the good in your partner, not the weaknesses.

Often after I have listened to the terrible description of an obvious ogre of a husband I ask the angry woman, "How did an intelligent lady like you ever get attracted to such a loser? What did you see in him in the first place?"

Usually her response is, "Well, he used to be different. When I first met him he was handsome, witty, generous . . ."

"What caused this all to change?"

"Not everything changed. He's actually still good-looking if he'd ever smile. He can be funny at parties, though he's dull as dishwater at home. He's still generous with the kids, but he wouldn't give me a nickel."

It's always easy for an outsider to see that there are still good points in this man, but she seems to bring out the worst in him. Is he really such a rat? What is there that is positive about this person?

In Philippians 4:8 Paul directs our attention to a checklist of the good in others: "Finally, brothers, whatever is true, whatever is noble, whatever is right, whatever is pure, whatever is lovely, whatever is admirable—if anything is excellent or praiseworthy—think about such things" (NIV).

When you read this over, can you find something true, noble, right, pure, lovely, or admirable about your mate? Is there any excellence? Anything worthy of praise? Let your mind dwell and think on these things. Then ask the Father to give you a new vision of your mate. Ask Him to let you see your mate the way He sees them. Ask the Lord to remove your old perceptions and give you new sight for your mate. Thank the Father for your husband/wife and for the positive things you see in him or her.

❧

Memorize Philippians 4:8 and begin to dwell on the good in your mate. Ask the Holy Spirit to help you take every thought captive (2 Corinthians 10:5) that is not true, noble, right, pure, lovely, admirable, excellent, or praiseworthy.

The Cure for Marriage Problems

7. Forget the past.

So many marriages are doomed forever because of past mistakes. The partners are unforgiving and are constantly digging up what happened ten years ago. Whenever a disagreement arises they reach into their bag of tricks and find their two favorite words: always and never. *Always* goes with everything bad and *never* goes with everything good, such as:

"You are *always* late."

"You *never* say a kind word." The past becomes so much a part of today that there is no hope for the future.

Years from now we'll still be trudging down this dreary trail because we've *always* had problems and things will *never* get better. When you look at these thoughts on paper, you can easily see that a constant review of the past precludes any improvement in the future. Yet there is hope once we realize the rut we are in and want to rise out of it. Paul says, "The one thing I do . . . is to forget what is behind me and do my best to reach what is ahead" (Philippians 3:13 TEV).

Basically Paul is saying that if we are reaching forward we must forget what is behind! We cannot hold on to the past (looking at it, being consumed with it, constantly bringing it up) and be focused and reaching toward what is ahead! Paul emphasized that it was the "one thing" he did! That is how important it was for Paul to forget the past and move on! And it is that important for us today, especially in our marriages! We must get rid of the past in order to live for the future. How? We must be *willing* to let it go.

As Christians, we have the power to forget the past when we are willing. "If any man be in Christ, he is a new creature: old things are passed away; behold, all things are become new" (2 Corinthians 5:17). There may be a memory, but it will have no sting and no power to destroy our lives.

❧

*Are you allowing the past to keep you in bondage?
Is the past still a hindrance in your marriage? Do
you angrily recall things from your mate's past?
Once you have forgiven your mate, you must choose
to allow him to be the "new creation" God has
made. Don't keep that shackle of the past around
your mate's ankles. Set your mate free—it will set
you free.*

The Cure for Marriage Problems

8. Believe that God can help you and thank Him ahead of time for what He is going to do in your life.

Do you really believe that God *knows* you? Do you believe that He *knows* the hairs on your head? Do you believe that not a sparrow falls without His *knowing?* The Bible assures us that God *knows* His children. A father wants the best for his family and will give his children all he has.

Those of us who are parents are always thrilled when our children appreciate us, when they say thanks.

Several times during Marita's teen years when she fussed because we wouldn't let her do a certain thing, she returned later to say, "Thank you for saying no." In the same way our Father loves to hear thanks from His children even when we are not enthused over our circumstances. We're here for a reason, and only our Father can weave together our past, our present, and our future.

"In every thing give thanks: for this is the will of God in Christ Jesus concerning you" (1 Thessalonians 5:18).

What is your problem today? Are you ready to take action?

Will you DECIDE to improve the situation?

Will you EXAMINE yourself and not your mate?

Are you big enough to CONFESS your weaknesses
as sin?

Do you care enough to ASK God to rid you of your
faults?

Can you really FORGIVE your partner and
apologize?

Are you willing to LOOK at the good in your mate?

Do you want to FORGET the past and its bad
memories?

Do you BELIEVE that God can help you, and will
you THANK Him ahead of time for what He's
going to do in your life?

❧

Simple steps to a satisfactory solution!

Becoming a Better Man

Men, do you realize that God has personally appointed you to be the spiritual head of your household?

What an overwhelming thought—a divine appointment! But are you ready for it? Do you think you have to wear a white robe and a tinsel halo, move the family to a monastery, or mumble a mantra?

Let's see what Peter has to say to the man of today.

"Likewise, ye husbands, dwell with them according to knowledge, giving honor unto the wife, as unto the weaker vessel, and as being heirs together of the grace of life; that your prayers be not hindered" (1 Peter 3:7).

Likewise—the connector between words to the women and to the men.

Ye husbands—listen, it's for you!

Dwell with them—live with your own wife, not somewhere else.

How?

According to knowledge—spiritual understanding of your role in marriage.

Giving honor to the wife—treating her with respect and courtesy.

As unto the weaker vessel—know that she needs your leadership and covering.

As being heirs together of the grace of life—equal in God's sight.

Why?

That your prayers be not hindered—to experience answered prayer.

Becoming a better man is not easy, but it is the most important thing you can do for your wife and children. God has entrusted you with a wonderful responsibility to cover and protect your family. And remember, Christ is covering you as you lead your family spiritually.

❧

Men, meditate and memorize 1 Peter 3:7. Decide in your heart that you are going to be the spiritual leader of your family that God has called you to be. Thank God that you will operate in headship, not Lordship. Ask the Holy Spirit to give you a hunger for the Word of God and then to teach you how to be a better husband, father, and person.

Insecure Men

To honor your wife means to treat her with respect, be courteous, use good manners. I've met many men who were gallant gentlemen at work and offensive oafs at home.

Fred and I were recently invited to a couple's home for dinner. When we arrived the husband greeted us with, "That poor dummy hasn't got anything ready yet." Before we were inside the door, he had communicated to us that he was married to some dull incompetent who was probably not going to be able to get dinner on the table at all.

As we began to observe their relationship, we could see why the poor thing was under pressure. He was standing over her, nagging her every inch of the way, pointing out what she was doing wrong, and not helping her at all. "Why don't you hurry up? They're sitting there waiting! Why don't you put the bread on the table? What's wrong with you, anyway? The peas are boiling. You know I hate peas when they boil. You've got the butter too near the burner and it's melting. Why can't you ever do anything right?"

Fred and I were embarrassed and wished we'd never come. McDonald's would have been marvelous compared to this chronicle of criticism.

Men, when you try to convince others of your competence by cutting down your wife, what you are really saying is, "I am an insecure man who hopes to cover up my inferiority complex by browbeating my wife into abject submission so you'll be impressed with my strength." How we want to flee from that type of a rude, insensitive brute who has to build his ego at the expense of others!

❧

What about you? Do you honor your wife? If you find yourself relating to the husband in the above story, go to the Father and ask Him to change you. Deal with your own insecurities so that you can truly love, honor, and cherish your wife.

"Such confidence as this is ours through Christ before God. Not that we are competent to claim anything for ourselves, but our COMPETENCE comes from God" (Romans 3:4 NIV).

Husbands, Please Notice!

A wife who is genuinely admired by her husband will not run off to seek approval. Notice your wife's clothes, her hairstyle, and her makeup, and encourage her.

"When he tells me I look good, I want to look better."

"His compliments keep me taking care of myself."

"He never noticed what I wore so I don't bother to dress up anymore."

A bright Sally Sanguine came up to me one day just before I went in to speak to a group of husbands. She said, "Tell those men that if they're too dumb to compliment their wives, at least be smart enough not to compliment other women in their presence." She then dumped this story on me. "At Christmas we were going to the office party for my husband's business. I bought a new red velvet dress, had my hair done up in an elegant style, and got sparkly eye shadow. When I walked out of the bedroom to leave, I could hardly wait for his reaction. I should have waited. He glanced at me and said, 'You're late.' I stood in shock as he threw my coat over my shoulders and walked to the car. Neither of us said a word. We got to the party and walked in the door, and he spotted my friend Jean. His whole personality changed. 'Jean, my love, how gorgeous you look! Your dress fits like a glove, and your hair is soft. Wow! I can't take my eyes off you.'"

You can imagine Sally's reaction—she was furious. "Why don't they notice a thing we wear and then fall all over a stray girl who doesn't even look that good?" Why, men, why?

Admire what's admirable, and we'll work to improve. Ignore us, and we'll quit trying.

During the low period of our marriage, I felt unloved and insignificant. Fred only noticed what was wrong with me, and mentally I ran away. I went out to find myself years before most women knew they were lost. I got jobs that always put me on center stage, where people had to look up and notice me. If I got enough compliments during the day I could stand Fred at night. Gratefully, all that is changed now, and Fred makes me feel that I'm the most important part of his life. When I know I am a person of significance for Fred, I don't need to hear words of praise from other men.

Some of you may be thinking, "If you could only see my wife you'd agree there's nothing there to admire." All the more reason to hunt, for she must really need to be uplifted.

❧

There is always something in the worst of us to be praised, and the less lovely a person is the more he or she needs encouragement.

To Be Admonished

To admonish means to reprove gently and kindly. Even if you were a perfect man trying to organize a perfect family, there would be times when your wife got so far out of hand that you would need to pull her back in line. How do you handle this touchy task?

The quickest way is to yell at her immediately in front of the kids and show them all who's boss.

You could wait until she's about to do the same thing again and remind her firmly how badly she botched this before.

You could hover over her as often as possible and watch for impending doom.

All of these ideas are guaranteed to make her fall somewhere between discouraged and defiant. So how do you tell her that something has to be done differently? You could do what Fred did.

The problem: We had a Bible study in our home each Tuesday evening. Fred wanted dinner early on Tuesdays so we could be cleaned up before the guests arrived. I never seemed to remember when it was Tuesday, and Fred came home ready to eat and I wasn't even there. When I arrived, we would throw something together quickly, wolf it down, clean up in a hurry, and welcome our friends with the peace of the Lord in our hearts, right?

What could Fred do about me? He took me out for

lunch, and while I was so grateful for this oasis in a busy day, he began to compliment me.

"You accomplish more in a given day than any woman I know. How you write, speak, teach, travel, and run a home is beyond me. Because of how well you do and how much you have on your mind, I hate to add one more pressure to your life. However, do you think it is possible to have some simple supper on the table by 5:30 on Tuesdays?"

When Fred approached the problem this way, I wanted to be a part of the solution. When he said he knew it was too much to ask, I wanted to show him I could do it. We worked it out. He let me know when it was Tuesday—that was the biggest help right there—and I got home on time. He was happy with some light meal and he helped me clean up. We even had time to sit down and review our lesson before the doorbell rang.

❦

Men, the best of us women will make mistakes, but with a positive approach from you we will try to improve.

A Changed Fred

After thirteen years of marriage, when Fred gave his heart to Jesus and began to truly change, I had a difficult time totally believing what was happening. As Fred continued to show me unconditional love for the first time in our marriage, I was doubtful that his changes would last. One day I decided to test him. I called his office and said, "Fred, I need you at home immediately."

"I'll be right there," he replied and hung up. I quickly dialed back to tell him I was just kidding, but he had already left. I spent a dreadful ten minutes trying to work up an emergency, but I couldn't come up with one. I ran out to the car as he drove up and confessed that there was no problem. I was just testing him. I expected either a blowup or a lecture, but instead he said, "I don't blame you."

I knew that Fred had changed, but I pretended I didn't notice.

One day Fred took my Ford to be fixed and left me his Lincoln. As I got in his car, I saw a three-by-five card taped to the dashboard. On it was printed: PRAISE FLO.

For the first time my heart began to melt. I realized that it had been so hard for him to find something good to say about me that he had needed to put up a reminder. I sat in the car and cried.

For one year I resisted Fred's new charm, I tested

his new sincerity, and I pretended not to notice his changes. I was cold and unresponsive. I was not going to forgive or forget thirteen years of emotional torture so easily.

But Fred was willing to love me unconditionally, expecting nothing in return, and eventually I realized that the change in his life was real.

I knelt down beside my bed and asked God to cause me to fall in love with my husband. When I was willing, He was able.

Don't be discouraged, men, if you make all the improvements and she seems unwilling to respond. Years of hurt feelings can't be repaired overnight. You be the one to start. Show her that she comes first in your life, and she won't be able to resist you.

> *When your wife is doubtful of your love she'll demand things.*
>
> *When she knows you love her unconditionally, she won't care what else she owns.*
>
> *When you are a loving husband you will produce a pleasing wife.*

❦

Let us not be weary in well doing: for in due season we shall reap, if we faint not" (Galatians 6:9).

REMEMBER: *If you want heaven at eleven start before seven!*

David's Cry

No good Christian woman gets up in the morning, looks out the window, and says, "My, this is a lovely day! I guess I'll go out and commit adultery." Yet I've talked to many who did it anyway. No good Christian man wants to abandon his family for a clandestine relationship. Yet the "other woman" is a national problem.

A few years ago I would never have thought that the subject of adultery was anything to mention in a Christian book. I was brought up to believe that nice girls didn't even think about such things. As a teenager I not only didn't succumb to temptations but I didn't even know there were any. I got married two weeks before my twenty-fifth birthday, innocent and pure as the driven snow. I hadn't even read a dirty book.

In these days when even Miss Piggy is passionate, my life nestles in with *Little House on the Prairie*. Then how did I begin to speak on the subject of adultery? It was an accident. A few years ago I wrote a lesson on forgiveness and used the story of David as an example. As I studied David I found a good man who got into trouble, much like Eve (a good woman who didn't mean to go astray).

David was a spiritual giant who knew the Scriptures and taught them to others. He was handsome, talented, musical, poetic, and regal, yet he violated three of the ten commandments. He coveted his neighbor's wife, committed adultery, and plotted the murder of her husband. When the enormity of his sin engulfed him, he cried out to God for forgiveness.

In 2 Samuel chapter 11 we see how David, a man after God's own heart, went astray. Perhaps you've followed these same steps.

How do good people get into trouble?

1. They aren't where God wants them to be.
2. Temptation comes along.
3. They commit the sin.
4. They feel guilty.
5. The cover-up gets them in deeper.
6. They eventually get caught.
7. God forgives.
8. But they are punished.

Does the Bible have advice? Yes. David gives it himself in Psalm 51, written after his visit with Nathan (the one used by God to confront David with his sin). David knew he had sinned, and he cried out to God.

Have you yielded to temptation? Have you stepped into trouble with your eyes wide open? Perhaps you've strayed from the straight and narrow.

What do you do when you've already strayed? Try David's advice. Read and meditate on Psalm 51 today.

No Pot So Black . . .

A person who never admits being wrong and is self-righteous is unattractive to others, but one who is willing to admit his sin and the depth of God's forgiving power has much to share with others. When I was young and cocky, thinking I could control my destiny, I had no compassion for people with problems. I felt that mistakes were a sign of weakness, and I respected only strength.

Once I suffered through the loss of my two sons, after doing everything humanly possible to heal them, I knew what heartbreak was, and I could feel for others.

Once I was brought to my knees with a broken spirit, I was open to the claims of Christ and I was restored. The Lord Jesus gave me a new life to use for His glory.

David told God, in essence, "When this is over, I'll teach others about You, and many will be converted" (Psalm 51:13).

Why not make the best of your worst? What problem are you involved in right now? Follow the good advice David gave in Psalm 51:

1. Ask God for mercy.
2. Admit your mistake.
3. Tell the truth.

4. Clean up your act.
5. Restore fellowship with God and your partner.
6. Ask for the joy of the Lord.
7. Thank God for your broken spirit.
8. Teach others from your mistakes and bring them to the Lord.

There is no pot so black that God can't shine it up and use it for His glory!

❧

Have you seen your failures as the end of being used by God? As you follow David's good advice, ask God to give you a fresh perspective on how He can use your painful mistakes to help others.

"And the Lord said, 'Simon, Simon! Indeed, Satan has asked for you, that he may sift you as wheat. But I have prayed for you, that your faith should not fail; and when you have returned to Me, strengthen your brethren'" (Luke 22:31–32 NKJV).

Why Have I Built These Walls?

According to the dictionary, communication is a sharing of ideas, an exchange of information, a mutual participation. Using this basis, communication is not a monologue, a tirade, or a deaf ear.

We are usually attracted to someone who communicates with us on the same wavelength. We have mutual interests. We love to hear about the other person's activities, we enjoy sharing on verbal and emotional levels. We think that if we marry, we will live and communicate happily ever after.

What went wrong? When did your communication break down? Did one of you talk so much that the other quit listening? Did you find that your opinion just didn't matter? Were you proven wrong with facts every time you tried to discuss a meaningful issue? Did you become afraid of your partner's reaction to touchy subjects—afraid you'd be corrected or laughed at?

All of these genuine concerns push us farther apart, and some of our marriages deteriorate into two people living under the same roof but with not much in common. We have built walls between us.

In marriage no one loves a wall, and yet many of us are as busy as beavers building barriers that effectively block out our communication.

What barriers have you built to block communications? Have you walled yourself away from your mate

so there is no mutual participation? Can you talk to
your hairdresser more freely than to your mate?

Ask yourself these questions:

1. Do I interrupt and finish sentences for others?
2. Do I drop into depression as a defense?
3. Do I get angry if people don't see things my way?
4. Do I pretend to agree just to shut them up, and
   resent it inside?
5. Do I make a joke out of serious subjects in order
   to avoid facing them?
6. Do I make fun of others and ridicule them in
   front of people?
7. Do I jump to my own defense before anyone
   can plead a case?
8. Do I clam up and refuse to talk when the subject
   gets too close?

❧

*If you have answered yes to even a few of these,
you have trouble communicating. You may be verbal
and vivacious, but if you use any of these blocks you
are walling yourself away from a true exchange of
ideas with those close to you.*

*Ask the Holy Spirit to help you understand why
you have built walls and for help in tearing them
down.*

Communication Guidelines: Dealing with Men

It is absolutely essential that couples talk things out with each other if they wish to have a rich, deep, and meaningful marriage.

Hugh Boudreau, a Baltimore marriage counselor, said, "The inability of husbands and wives to talk to each other is our number one marriage problem."

Women, this is what a *man* wants:

1. *Sincerity*—When women converse we tend to fill in the cracks with excuses and with blame put on others, but our husbands would like sincere statements. When we communicate with them they would like us to be sincere with no guile, artifice, or fillers.
2. *Simplicity*—A man desires an open heart, a clear statement, an honest answer—an uncomplicated truth. We often cover and conceal. We drench them with details and drown them in trivia.
3. *Sensitivity*—As women we must be sensitive to our partner's needs and not approach him with our problems when it is clearly not the right time. So often we store up complaints in a bottle all day and when our husband walks in we take out the stopper and let him have it.

When this deluge becomes a constant style of communication, our mates stop coming home or arrive with plugs in their ears.

4. *Stability*—Many men tell me they are afraid to bring up any meaningful subject to their wives because they fall apart. Men don't like weepy women, and if a woman employs this type of barrier to communication often enough, her husband will withdraw.

    Men like to approach problems from an organized, businesslike point of view, and they respect a woman who is stable and serene even under stress.

❧

Ladies, pray that God will give you the sincerity, simplicity, sensitivity, and stability to communicate more effectively with your husbands.

Communication Guidelines: Dealing with Women

In the previous devotional we discussed what a man needs in communication. Now let's look at what a woman needs.

Men, this is what a woman wants:

1. *Attention*—All of us crave attention so much that if you won't listen to our heartfelt pleas, we will find someone who will.

   If you want to communicate with us, pay attention to what we say but don't feel we need answers. Fred finally understands that when I cry out my problems to him, I only want him to listen and commiserate. I don't want him to prescribe a cure. I already know the answer; I just want an audience.

   To communicate with us, listen to us and love us. Don't preach or teach. Answer only if we ask, and even then proceed with caution.

2. *Agreement*—If you men want to open up communications, try to agree with us in some area quickly. This will unnerve us and give you an immediate advantage. Because most of you love to argue with us and put us down, we are stunned by a man who agrees with us on anything.

3. *Appreciation*—The dictionary tells us that appreciation implies "a just estimation of a thing's value; an understanding." Oh, how we women want to be looked upon as something of value, and how we want to know that you understand what we are trying to say!

   We won't always be logical and we won't think as you do, but we do want to be appreciated and understood.

4. *Appointments*—When you men sense that there are some communication problems in your marriage, take the leadership role and set aside some special time to converse. Who knows what little irritants you could clear up if you tried? Make an appointment with your wife and learn to communicate.

❧

Men, ask God to help you give your wife attention, agreement, appreciation, and appointments so that you are able to communicate more effectively.

Private Property

Many times we make it difficult for our mates to communicate with us. Often we let them play guessing games until they smash into the concrete walls that we have erected in our lives.

One day I was visiting in a small town, and as I drove down the street to the home where I was staying, I noticed one yard with a big sign on it that said "Private Property—Keep Out." A big, ugly dog was chained to the sign, and my curiosity was aroused. What's different about this house? What kind of people live there? What made them put up the sign and send out the dog? No other house on the street attracted my attention except the one labeled "Private Property." I asked my hostess about it and she told me the couple there hated children and put up the sign to let people know this. "The strange thing is," she said, "that all the children are drawn to that yard. They walk as close to the property as they dare, they throw things at the dog, and they ruin the place on Halloween."

By putting "Private Property" on their lawn, this couple had aroused the curiosity and attention of all who passed by. We always want to know about whatever is off-limits. Let's think about this story with regard to communication with our mates.

Ask yourself, "What private property am I protecting?"

1. Am I covering up my past and not willing to share my childhood, my family, my ambitions, my hurts, and my defeats with my partner?
2. Am I eaten up inside because I'm hiding a big secret that needs to be dealt with?
3. Am I unable to discuss money problems and work them through without becoming emotional?
4. Am I unwilling to cooperate on raising the children, and am I putting the blame for failures on my mate?
5. Am I afraid to let anyone get to know my real self, or am I not sure who I really am?
6. Am I an expert at avoiding anything that demands action?

Go ahead and get rid of your "private property" areas with your mate. These areas will hinder your marriage by stifling communication. Take down the sign and get rid of the dog . . . . it's only making matters worse.

Pause at this point and assess your marriage communication problems. Remember, it takes two to communicate, and one must lead. As a start, find a time when you and your mate can discuss your mutual problems. Ask the Holy Spirit to help you break down the barriers that keep you from communicating on a positive level.

In the Light

We can try to break down the barriers to communication with our own hands, but we will fail. "All we like sheep have gone astray; we have turned every one to his own way" (Isaiah 53:6). When our own way leads us into trouble, when our marriage is falling apart, we little sheep need help. When a wall has come up between us and we're talking through the cracks, we need a carpenter to take it down. We need Jesus. Jesus broke down the communication barrier between Fred and me.

As Fred teaches, "My peace does not depend on my partner's behavior but on my relationship with the Lord." Where are you today? Are you and your partner on opposite sides of a wall? Is there a middle wall of partition between you? Are you tired of talking through a hole in the wall? It takes one person to start the upward climb. Shouldn't it be you?

Look Up

"Thou wilt keep him in perfect peace, whose mind is stayed on thee: because he trusteth in thee" (Isaiah 26:3).

Know that when you look up to the Lord and trust Him to straighten out your problem with your partner, He will. You are responsible for your own behavior, not his. Do what you know is right, and let the Lord pull up your mate.

Lift Up

"If I be lifted up . . . [I] will draw all men unto me" (John 12:32).

When you lift up the Lord and not yourself and your opinions, you take the pressure off your partner and allow the Lord to work. He will, in His own time and way, draw your partner to Himself.

Light Up

"For he is our peace, who hath made both one, and hath broken down the middle wall of partition between us" (Ephesians 2:14).

❧

Let Christ lift you both up to the top and make you one again. Let Jesus reunite you with a peace that passes all understanding. Ask Him to break down the middle wall of partition between you, so you see the light. Thank Him that no longer are you each huddled in darkness on opposite sides of the wall, but you are together, on top, in the light.

Throw Out the Jars!

Are you a person who struggles with depression? Do you feel like you have a little black cloud (some of you may have huge storm clouds!) always hanging over your head? Obviously, there are many different reasons and degrees of depression as well as steps to overcoming depression. However, I want to point out a simple suggestion that seems to have helped many a depression-bound person get his or her thoughts on a positive level.

In my book, *Blow Away the Black Clouds* (that thoroughly deals with the subject of depression), I describe how one of the steps that helps a person start blowing away that dark cloud of depression is to get organized.

What can you do to get organized? Perhaps you are depressed because you have never finished the housework. Nothing has ever been perfect. I've been married forty-two years and have never risen clearly above the waters, but with organization, the swimming is easier.

Let's pretend your house is a mess right now and you know it's hopeless. What a great basis for eternal depression! Why not set a reasonable goal? Clean one room a day for as long as you have rooms. Write this schedule down and then start. Just seeing in print that you will have a clean house a week from Tuesday will lift your spirits.

Start with the kitchen. Take everything out of one cabinet at a time. Put all the odd glasses and jelly jars in a box for the church rummage sale and buy some matching ones at K-Mart. Put covers on all the refrigerator jars and then throw out the jars and covers that have no mates. This act alone will give you an empty shelf. Stuff all the odd plastic plates and spoons into a box labeled "Good for Picnics"—in case you ever have one—and put it in the garage. Throw out the torn placemats and turn the faded tablecloths into dustcloths. Check your canned goods and throw away the six cans of artichoke hearts you bought on sale and are afraid to serve your family. Give your neighbor the big bag of dog food you bought the week before Spot died. Do you get the idea? By the time you finish the kitchen, you will be deliriously happy and ready to tackle your bedroom closet in the morning. What a productive way to overcome depression! Let all things be done decently and in order (1 Corinthians 14:40 NKJV).

❧

For those of you who have never tried this organized road to ecstasy, perhaps you should put this book down and start cleaning! Are you willing to get organized? Make a list of the areas in your life that need to be pulled together.

Personalities:
Who Am I?

People are always interested in analyzing themselves. We all want to know, "Who am I?" This eternal question has been asked by the ancient philosophers, the Jewish patriarchs, and the Renaissance man. It is the major question college students discuss and ponder, and is of such concern to adults today that I have spent twenty-two years of seminar teaching helping people to find answers.

Oswald Chambers said, "Personality is that peculiar, incalculable thing that is meant when we speak of ourselves as distinct from everyone else. Our personality is always too big for us to grasp. An island in the sea may be but the top of a great mountain. Personality is like an island, we know nothing about the great depths underneath, consequently we cannot estimate ourselves."

Our personality is too big for us to grasp, and it is difficult to estimate ourselves. Yet there is one theory of personality evaluation that has been around for over two thousand years.

The four temperaments were first labeled by Hippocrates, a noted Greek philosopher and physician and author of the Hippocratic oath taken by the medical profession over the years. As he dealt with complex human problems, he felt it would help people to understand themselves if he could simplify their personality traits and label them. Using the fluids of the body as types he said the *Sanguine* (blood) was the talker who wanted to have fun. The *Choleric* (yellow bile) was the worker who wanted to be in control. The *Melancholy* (black bile) was the thinker who wanted everything perfect. The *Phlegmatic* (phlegm) was the balancer of life who wanted to keep peace and avoid conflict.

When Fred and I first came across this theory in 1968, it revolutionized our marriage. I had always thought he was the only person in the world who reasoned that if you could only make out a chart on any given problem, you could solve it rationally. He thought I was the only one who felt it was more important to enjoy myself than to get the details down perfectly. When I learned that he was Melancholy and there were thousands like him, I backed up and looked at him in a new light. When he found out that I was Sanguine and that having fun didn't mean I was without purpose, he relaxed his grip on my training program. For the first time in fifteen years of marriage, we began to accept each other as we were, not as we had always hoped the other would become.

❧

Ask the Holy Spirit to teach you what you need to know from this material on personalities.

Personalities: Key Points

In our seminars we use the knowledge of the temperaments for two purposes:

1. To examine our own strengths and weaknesses and learn how to accentuate the positive and eliminate the negative.
2. To help us understand other people and realize that just because someone is different that does not make him wrong.

As you come to understand your own characteristics, there are a few key points to remember:

1. *Labels are not important.* Our objective is to see that we have certain God-given strengths and weaknesses. We are not trying to categorize everyone into neat packages.
2. *Each of us is different.* We are unique individuals. As we all have different thumbprints, so we all have different temperament blends.
3. *No one is 100 percent.* Each one of us is a combination of temperament traits. For example, I am 50-50 Sanguine-Choleric.
4. *Testing is for self-analysis only.* We study temperaments to understand ourselves. Our function is not to label each other.

5. *No one temperament is better than another.* Temperaments are natural, God-given traits.

6. *We do not seek to change our temperament.* However, by understanding our weaknesses, we can work prayerfully to obliterate them from our lives.

7. *Opposites attract.* Focusing on our partner's strengths allows compatibility while concentrating on our differences causes trouble.

8. *The Holy Spirit is at work in us.* It is the Holy Spirit of God who is constantly at work in us to transform us into the image of what He wants us to be. The Holy Spirit can enhance our strengths and overcome our weaknesses.

9. *God uses all four personality types.* Once we examine ourselves and stop trying to reshape others, we open our hearts to change. When we realize that others can be different and yet not be wrong, our relationships improve. The variety of natures is what adds spice to life as each of us sees the same event from a different point of view.

❧

Take the time to prayerfully understand the positive impact that understanding the various temperaments will bring to your relationships. Ask the Father to give you understanding as you proceed through the Personalities Section.

Personalities:
Unique Parts of the Body

As Fred and I began to share how the Lord had taken knowledge of the temperaments and revolutionized our marriage, we could see that the theory worked. People who thought there was no hope that they would ever understand each other suddenly looked at each other with clear eyes. We began to search our hearts and analyze ourselves, using the tool of the temperaments. As we brought couples into our home and shared what little we knew, we saw changes in ourselves and others. We saw how God has made us each so uniquely.

We learned God did not make us all alike. Each one of us is unique. Paul tells us that we should examine ourselves and find out what gifts God has given us, and what weaknesses He wishes us to overcome with our willingness and His power. Paul compares us to a body where Christ is the head and we are the parts. "Under his control all the different parts of the body fit together, and the whole body is held together by every joint with which it is provided. So when each separate part works as it should, the whole body grows and builds itself up through love" (Ephesians 4:16 TEV).

God made each one of us different, so we could function in our own role. He made some of us to be *feet*—to move, to administer, to accomplish, like the Choleric. He made some of us to be *minds*—to think deeply, to feel, to write, like the Melancholy. He made some of us to be *hands*—to serve, to smooth, to soothe, like the Phlegmatic. He made some of us to be *mouths*—to talk, to teach, to encourage, like the Sanguine. "Now hath God set the members every one of them in the body, as it hath pleased him" (1 Corinthians 12:18).

God could have made us all Sanguines. We would have lots of fun but accomplish little.

He could have made us all Melancholies. We would have been organized and charted but not very cheerful.

He could have made us all Cholerics. We would have been all set to lead but impatient that no one would follow.

He could have made us all Phlegmatics. We would have had a peaceful world but not much enthusiasm for life.

We need each temperament for the total function of the body. Each part should do its work to unify the action and produce harmonious results.

❧

Thank the Father that you have been fearfully and wonderfully made by Him. Thank Him for designing you with a purpose and for giving you the gifts and personality that you need to fulfill it. Meditate on Psalm 139:14–16.

The Sanguine:
"O Flo"

The most obvious way to spot a Sanguine is by listening in on any group and locating the one who is the loudest and chatting the most constantly. While the other temperaments talk, Sanguines tell stories.

When we lived in New Haven, Connecticut, the city built a seven-story parking garage. One day before Christmas, I parked my car in this gray cement structure that looked somewhat like an open penitentiary and went off to do my shopping. Sanguines, being circumstantial people with short memories, have difficulty in locating misplaced items, such as cars, and when I walked out of Macy's and faced this foreboding fortress, I had no idea where I'd left my car.

True to Sanguine form, I stood staring up at the seven stories and wondered where I should start. A handsome young man walked by, noticed I was bewildered holding an armload of bundles, and asked, "What's your trouble, honey?"

"I lost my car in this seven-story garage."

"What kind of a car is it?"

"Well, that's part of the problem—I don't know."

"You don't know what kind of a car you own?" he asked in disbelief.

"Well, we own two, and I don't know which one I drove today."

He thought for a minute and then said, "Let me see your keys, and I can narrow it down."

That was no easy request, because I had to set down all my packages and empty out my entire handbag on the curb before I found two sets of car keys. By this time, another man, seeing me on my knees in the gutter, asked, "What's the matter here?"

The first man said, "She's lost her car in the seven-story parking garage."

He asked the same question: "What kind of a car is it?"

"She doesn't know."

"She doesn't know? Then how can we ever find it?"

I explained before they both gave up. "It's either a yellow convertible with black insides and red dials, or a large, navy blue car with matching velour seats."

They both shook their heads, picked up my packages, and led me off to the parking garage. As we searched seven stories, other helpful souls attached themselves to our group, and we became acquainted. By the time we found the yellow convertible with the license plate O FLO we were such good buddies, I wanted to start a club and be president!

✄

Being cheerful keeps you healthy (Proverbs 17:22, TEV).

The Sanguine:
"Coffee and Corn"

Since Sanguines want to be helpful and popular, they volunteer without much thought. One night as Fred and I were teaching temperaments to a group in New York, I mentioned how Sanguines volunteer and don't follow through. "For example," I said, "if a Sanguine had volunteered to make the coffee for our break tonight, we would find that she had forgotten even to plug in the pot." At that point, an adorable, bright-eyed girl in the front row screamed, ran up the aisle, and disappeared into the kitchen. She was a Sanguine; she had volunteered to make the coffee; she had never plugged in the pot, and we had nothing to drink that night. Sanguines love to volunteer, and they mean well, but if you want coffee, you'd better plug it in yourself! However, when they do follow through, they do everything with a flair.

The Sanguine has an unconscious ability to turn any simple task into a main event. One evening, as the whole family was gathered in the living room at our daughter Lauren's home, Marita decided to make pop-corn. She jumped up and left for the kitchen, followed by four-year-old Randy. About ten minutes later, little Randy came running into the living room with his eyes round and bright like headlights.

"Come see the popcorn. It's shooting all over the place!"

We ran into the kitchen to see popcorn exploding like fluffy rockets out of the top of an air popper. We all grabbed bowls and tried to catch corn as it shot by. Marita had poured too much corn into the new air popper, turned it on, and left for the bathroom, leaving Randy in charge. The mistake turned into a hilarious party game as we all chased the airborne corn, and little Randy thinks Aunt Marita's kind of corn is the only way to pop!

❦

Oh, how this world needs the Sanguine!

The lift of joy in times of trouble.

The touch of innocence in a jaded era.

The word of wit when we're weighted down.

The lift of humor when we're heavyhearted.

The ray of hope to blow away our black clouds.

The enthusiasm and energy to start over and over again.

The creativity and charm to color a drab day.

The simplicity of a child in complex situations.

The Melancholy:
"Thinker"

Before I understood the temperaments I did not appreciate people who weren't like me. I wanted the fun-and-games approach to life, and I was too preoccupied with myself to realize my deficiencies or want assistance. As I became self-analytical, I started to see that while I was a good front person, I didn't have much follow-through. I began to value Fred's depth, his sensitivity, his organization, his lists. I began to see a need for a true helpmate like Fred and for Melancholy friends who could see beneath the surface of life.

Even as a baby the Melancholy appears to be thinking deeply. When we adopted our son, Fred, we knew nothing about temperaments and didn't recognize his Melancholy nature. The caseworker told us he was a serious baby, that he never seemed to smile, and that at three months he appeared to be analyzing everyone who passed by. These traits have been consistent in his life. As a teenager, he was serious and reliable, and he was often annoyed by Marita's lighthearted attitude. He doesn't feel life is very funny and finds it impossible to smile in the morning. He still is introspective and analytical, and living in a family of strong extroverts has not changed his temperament pattern.

As an adult, the Melancholy is the thinking person, serious of purpose, dedicated to order and organization, and appreciative of beauty and intelligence. He doesn't dash off in search of excitement but analyzes the best plan for his life. Without the Melancholy, we would have little poetry, art, literature, philosophy, or symphonies. We would be missing the culture, refinement, taste, and talent so deep within the Melancholy natures. We would have fewer engineers, inventors, scientists; our ledgers might be lost, and our columns wouldn't balance.

The Melancholies are the soul, the mind, the spirit, the heart of humanity. Oh, how the world needs the Melancholy!

❧

A sensible man watches for problems ahead and prepares to meet them. The simpleton never looks, and suffers the consequences" (Proverbs 27:12, TLB).

The Melancholy:
"Toilet Paper Tip"

Many of the little things in life that I don't even notice are very important to Melancholies. Take the toilet paper for example. I used to put it on the roller whatever way it happened to go, until Fred pointed out I was doing it wrong. "What do you mean *wrong?*" I countered. "It has stayed up there, hasn't it?"

He sighed, "Yes, it stayed up but it's on wrong. You have it backwards."

Even staring, I couldn't see how toilet paper could be backwards, but he showed me that the paper should come off the front of the roll—not hang down the back against the wall where you would have to go hunting for it. I didn't think you had to hunt far, but I agreed to do it his way and worked at remembering.

Years later, when printed toilet paper came out, Fred was so excited to show me how the little flowers blossom correctly if you put the roll on right, but are looking face-to-face with the tiles if you put it on backwards. I had to agree it made sense, and he felt vindicated. Now when I go into a home and the paper's on wrong, I feel compelled to take it off and reverse it.

When Fred shares this example at our seminars, I am always amazed at the number of Melancholies who come up and thank him for making it clear to their mates that there is only one right way to hang toilet paper!

❦

Oh, how the world needs the Melancholy!

The depth to see into the heart and soul of life.

The artistic nature to appreciate the beauty of the world.

The talent to create a masterpiece where nothing existed before.

The ability to analyze and arrive at the proper solution.

The eye for detail while others do shoddy work.

The aim to finish what they start.

The pledge, "If it's worth doing, it's worth doing right."

The desire to do all things decently and in order.

The Choleric:
"In Charge"

The Choleric is the dynamic person who dreams the impossible dream and aims to reach the unreachable star. The Choleric is always aiming, reaching, succeeding. While the Sanguine is talking and the Melancholy is thinking, the Choleric is achieving. He is the easiest temperament to understand and get along with, as long as you live by his golden rule: "Do it *my* way NOW!"

The Cholerics are similar to the Sanguines in that they are both outgoing and optimistic. The Choleric can communicate openly with people, and he knows everything will turn out all right—as long as he's in charge. He gets more done than other temperaments, and he lets you know clearly where he stands.

One of the quickest ways to spot the powerful personality of the Cholerics is to catch them pointing to others and moving in close to add emphasis. We call our little grandson Bryan a two-fingered Choleric because he points his two index fingers at the same time. No one had to place Bryan on a stool and say, "Listen here, we want you to be strong and bossy, take control of everything you can get your hands on, point at everyone to make them feel insecure, and get right up into a person's face if you need to exert more authority." No, we didn't have to teach this to Bryan—he came with the knowledge prepackaged in his head. One day he and my husband were playing a game and Bryan made a wrong move. Fred, being a Melancholy couldn't allow even a three-year-old to make a mistake, and he said, "Bryan dear, you are wrong." Instantly, Bryan retorted, pointing with two fingers, "I am not wong. I am wight!"

❧

Oh, how this world needs the Choleric!

The firm control when others are losing theirs.

The cut of decision for foggy minds.

The grip of leadership to head us to the good.

The willingness to take a chance in a doubtful situation.

The confidence to hold true in the face of ridicule.

The independence to stand alone and be counted.

The road map to life when we've gone astray.

The Choleric: "Relax?"

The Choleric is a great worker, but on the negative side, he just can't relax. He goes full steam ahead so long that he can't quite throw the switch and turn himself off. Since Fred and I are both half-Choleric, you can imagine the activity we generate. If we sit down, we feel guilty. Life was made for constant achievements and production. We had to learn to relax.

Last year Fred and I decided we badly needed a rest. My brother Ron suggested an island in the Bahamas that is so remote we would be forced to relax. We flew off to this paradise where we planned to do nothing but rest.

We missed breakfast the first day. (By the time we got down the staff had left!) After breakfast on the second day, we went out to investigate the long, slim island. We were right in the center, and we found there were only two things to do: walk to the right or walk to the left. By lunchtime we'd done both.

After lunch Fred and I went to our room and sat on the edges of the twin beds. Fred took out a clipboard and legal pad and said, "I think it's about time we got this vacation organized. We'd better go to breakfast early before the staff quits. We'll take our time and get into our bathing suits at 9:30 A.M. We'll then walk to the left. Since we want to get a tan we'll lie on the beach until 11:00 A.M., when we'll come back to the room for lunch."

I nodded along as Fred wrote down our schedule accounting for every minute up to a 3:00 P.M. walk to the right.

At this point I realized what we were doing. The Cholerics in need of a rest were planning out each day, so that we wouldn't waste our vacation. Even though we knew why we had chosen a quiet place, it was so contrary to our natures to relax that we were planning how to make the most of our time!

Cholerics must realize they are heart-attack candidates, and they must learn to relax!

❧

Are you one who needs to just relax? Ask the Holy Spirit to help you understand your Choleric temperament, and then stop for rest!

"And on the seventh day God ended His work which He had done, and He rested on the seventh day from all His work which He had done"
(Genesis 2:2 NKJV).

The Phlegmatic:
"Balance"

Understanding temperaments is the first step in understanding people. If we can't see the innate differences in others and accept them as they are, we will think everyone not like us is at least slightly irregular.

We learn that for a family to have a variety of temperament traits provides a variety of activities and interest. God did not intend us all to be Sanguines. We'd have a lot of fun but never quite get organized. God did not make us all Choleric leaders. If He had, there would be none left to follow.

God did not want us all to be perfect Melancholies, for if things went wrong, we'd all be depressed.

God *did* create the Phlegmatics as special people to be the buffers for the emotions of the other three, to provide stability and balance. The Phlegmatic tones down the wild schemes of the Sanguine. The Phlegmatic refuses to get too impressed with the brilliant decisions of the Choleric. The Phlegmatic doesn't take too seriously the intricate plans of the Melancholy.

The Phlegmatic is the great leveler of us all, showing us, "It doesn't really matter that much." We are all part of a complex plan in which each temperament, when functioning properly, will fit into the right place and unite to form an exciting and balanced picture.

Oh, how the world needs the Phlegmatic!

The stability to stay straight on course.

The patience to put up with provokers.

The ability to listen while others have their say.

The gift of mediation, uniting opposite forces.

The purpose of peace at almost any price.

The compassion to comfort those hurting.

The determination to keep your head while all around are losing theirs.

The will to live in such a way that even your enemies can't find anything bad to say about you.

The Phlegmatic:
"No More Wishy-Washy"

The Phlegmatic's major fault is his apparent inability to make decisions. A Choleric stands over him with a pot of boiling water and asks quickly, "Do you want coffee or tea?" The automatic answer is "I don't care." The Phlegmatic feels he is being agreeable and can't understand why the Choleric pours the hot water over his head!

On a flight out of Norfolk, Virginia, the flight attendant announced over the PA system that we had three choices of entrees for lunch. "You may have seafood Newburg, pepper steak, or lasagna. We do not have enough of each for everyone, so some of you at the end should think of a second choice."

She then turned immediately to the Phlegmatic man who was in the first row with me and asked him, "Which entree would you like?" And he replied, "Whichever one you have left over." The flight attendant, being Choleric, said, "I don't have anything left over! You are the first person I've asked." She hovered over him, waiting for a decision. Then I spoke up and said, "I'll have the Newburg." He looked up and said, "I guess I'll have that one too."

The Phlegmatic's problem with making decisions is not that he is incompetent, but that he has made one great decision never to make any decisions. After all, if you don't make the decision, you're not held accountable for the outcome.

The Phlegmatic must practice making decisions and be willing to accept responsibility. The friends, workers, and mates of the Phlegmatic will rejoice when he is able to stand tall and be decisive. If you are a Phlegmatic and indecisive, say good-bye to the wishy-washy blues!

❧

When you fear to make a decision, remember there is One who can help you.

"For the Lord grants wisdom! . . . He shows how to distinguish right from wrong, how to find the right decision every time" (Proverbs 2:6, 9 TLB).

Personalities...
"Like Our Best Friend"

Have you ever had a friend whom you loved so much that you wanted to be with him all the time and get to know him better every day? Has his presence lit up your life so you felt energized, just being close? Have you cared so much for him that you were willing to bear his burdens and stand in for him in times of trouble? Have you watched him so closely and followed him so much that you've almost become like him? Jesus wants that kind of relationship with you.

Jesus wants you to get to know Him better by reading His words and talking to Him; He wants you to feel His power in your life so you can overcome your weakness. He wants you to realize He suffered, just as you do, and He wants you to spend so much time with Him that you become like Him.

If you wanted to become like Him, you would aim to amplify your strengths and eliminate your weaknesses, for Jesus had the best of each temperament. He had the storytelling gifts of the Sanguine, the depth and sensitivity of the Melancholy, the administrative ability of the Choleric, and the calm and peaceful nature of the Phlegmatic.

Jesus lives today in the hearts of all believers, so as you put your personal plan for improvement into action, make sure you're connected to the source of Power to make it all possible. "The LORD hath done great things for us" (Psalm 126:3).

❦

PERSONALITY PLUS POWER PRODUCES POSITIVE PEOPLE

God could have made us all Sanguines. We would have lots of fun but accomplish little.

He could have made us all Melancholies. We would have been organized and charted but not very cheerful.

He could have made us all Cholerics. We would have been set to lead, but impatient that no one would follow.

He could have made us all Phlegmatics. We would have had a peaceful world but not much enthusiasm for life.

We need each temperament for the total function of the body. Each part should do its work to unify the action and produce harmonious results.